Friends of All Creatures

To Matthew Evans

and

Chris Witebsky

with love

Cover illustration: Juana and Saint Martin de Porres

FRIENDS OF ALL CREATURES

By Rose Evans

illustrated by Valeria Evans

foreword by Dr. Catherine Roberts

Sea Fog Press, Inc.

P.O. Box 210056

San Francisco, CA 94121-0056

First edition   December 1984

Copyright © 1984   Rose and Valeria Evans

Library of Congress Catalog Card Number   84 - 90073

International Standard Book Number
Hardcover edition: 0-917507-00-2
Paperback edition: 0-917507-01-0

Sea Fog Press Inc.

P.O. Box 210056

San Francisco, CA 94121-0056

Contents

Acknowledgments

We encountered great kindness in the process of making this book. Our deep thanks are due to Dr. Michael Fox, to Lewis Regenstein, and most especially to Dr. Catherine Roberts, for her generous kindness and many helpful suggestions.

We are most grateful to Editorial Epoca of Mexico City for their gracious permission to quote from their superb biography, "Belisario Dominguez, Su Vida Y Epoca" by Blanca Dominguez de Diez Gutierrez.

We owe the greatest thanks to Adib al-Awar for his kindness and painstaking work in translating for us, from the Arabic, the poetry of Abu l'Ala.

Many thanks to Jack MacPhee for his valuable help in research on the enemies of bullfighting.

We must also mention the very helpful staff of the General Reference Desk of that excellent institution, the San Francisco Public Library. They were helpful with research beyond the call of duty. When we needed a hard-to-find book, they never failed to get it for us from somewhere.

Foreword

Our views about the universe and our place in it have undergone enormous changes in our time. The profound new ideas concerning the nature of reality proposed by physicists early in this century have been confirmed and supplemented, not least by astronomers, cosmologists, and biologists. Not only are we and our children learning new ways of viewing the world, but all of us, for better or worse, have to accomodate ourselves to an environment being continually altered by science and technology – whose further advance remains one of our highest priorities.

What do scientists now tell us about the universe? They say it is strange almost beyond belief. Some even assert that it is not a collection of separate, living or non-living objects at all but rather a web of continually changing energy patterns - a single, unbroken, living Whole, whose "parts" are but fluctuating ripples on an endless sea of energy. Even more remarkable, each part, in its own way, seems to reflect or contain the whole. Certain 20th century physicists, reminiscent of 17th and 18th century philosophers, see no clear-cut distinction between the observer and the observed; the universe, they say, appears to be a kind of looking-glass that mirrors, at least to some extent, the state of mind of the observer. Are the things that are seen then abstractions? Does consciousness pervade the whole? Does everything affect every other thing? Such bewildering notions, violating common sense, are following one another in rapid succession as scientists from different fields acquire more knowledge about reality.

The excitement of continually expanding scientific visions of the world has a powerful attraction all its own. Yet, in a sense, this represents a danger. Let us not be carried away by the assumption that only scientists reflecting upon scientific knowledge can discover the truth about the universe and how it works. We must not neglect the achievements of other human minds that have reflected upon the spiritual reality of the universe and what they believed to be the moral law that sustains the whole. This is not to say that current scientific pronouncements are devoid of spiritual or ethical content. Some scientists are envisaging a coming synthesis of science with religion, pointing to the similarity between modern physics and eastern spirituality and calling for more peace, harmony, and unity in a fragmented world. So far, however, they seem to have reflected but little on the full ethical scope of the religious perspective and what its effect upon the advance of science – particularly the science of life – might be.

For this reason one must welcome this little book, FRIENDS OF ALL CREATURES. In all ages, from ancient times down to the present, there have been men and women distinguished by a certain nobility of spirit expressing itself as a moral commitment to befriend the earth's defenceless creatures and to prevent their abuse. These courageous individuals, most of whom professed a particular faith, seem moved to action by deep spiritual insight into the common essence of all religions. In serving suffering beings, they disclosed the existence in the universe of a close relation between the human and the divine. Their intuitive sense of justice, compassion, and what is eternally right points   to the reality of a divine ethic that leads us on. Whether recognized as such or not, our present global concern for the living environment is a component of this spiritual ascent towards the Good.

FRIENDS OF ALL CREATURES may have a significant educational role in this time of bewildering new scientific visions of reality. It acquaints young and old alike with a religious vision of the good life that science tends to lack. In popular language, supplemented by many illustrations, this book recounts familiar and unfamiliar stories of men and women who, with little or no knowledge of 20th century science, nevertheless seemed able to glimpse the radiance of the Eternal Good and, in doing so, served both the parts and the Whole. In an age still dominated by science, we can all benefit from these stories, be we engaged in animal protectionism or environmentalism or in investigating the nature of the brain, mind, and consciousness by mutilating and destroying defenceless laboratory animals. Standing at the threshhold of a religious awakening, we can now look forward to a truer vision of our moral obligation to the living world.   Spiritual education can substantially transform the science of life. That biological and medical advance will one day be restrained by religious ethics seems inevitable. Rose and Valeria Evans' book may help to hasten this proper synthesis of science and religion. I hope it will be widely read.

Berkeley, 1984   Catherine Roberts

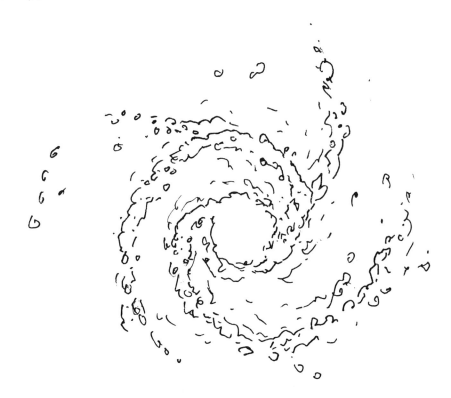

2

Preface

There has been a lot of joy in writing this book. Until I began work on it, I had no idea how many voices were raised to speak for the animals in the various cultures and religious communities, nor how close the connection is between the spiritual life and the spring of compassion.

This book is ecumenical, and includes people of all religions, and people who were associated with no organized religion. I was, originally, most familiar with animal friends in the Christian tradition. Several years of exploring other religions led me to the happy discovery that a serious concern for animals is a part of all great religions.

I have tried to keep this book positive and to emphasize the works of kindness. A book on this subject necessarily includes the mention of cruelty, but the central subject of the book is the good work of compassionate people.

I hope the lives of all these good people will inspire my readers to let the light of reverence for life shine in their lives, and that they will be moved to do the things they can do, each in his or her own way, to make the world a gentler place.

Moses carries a lost kid back to the flock

Moses

Moses was a shepherd in Midian, a kind protector of the flocks. He had come to Midian from Egypt, where his people lived under brutal slavery.

Moses narrowly escaped death as a baby. The Egyptian Pharaoh ordered all the boy babies of the Israelites killed, but his family hid him in a floating cradle and saved him.

As a young man, full of a fiery passion for justice, he killed an Egyptian slave driver who was beating a helpless Jewish worker. He had to flee for his life, so he went to Midian in Arabia.

When he came to Midian, he met seven sisters who were trying to care for the flocks of their father, Jethro. When they took their animals to the wells for water, the shepherds of the other flocks drove them away. Moses defended them and watered their animals for them. Then he married one of the sisters, Zipporah, and became the shepherd of Jethro's flocks.

The Midrash tells how Moses was chosen to be the leader of Israel because he was kind to the animals of his herd. A little goat ran away from the herd one day. Moses followed it until it came to a pool of water and drank. Moses said, "I didn't know you ran away because you were thirsty. You must be tired also". With that he picked up the little kid and carried it back. God said, "Because you have been merciful in tending this flock, as you live, you shall be the shepherd of my flock Israel".

And so it was. This brave man, Moses, returned to Egypt, went to the Pharaoh, and demanded that he free the Israelites. In the end, Moses led his people out of Egypt and through the Red Sea to freedom.

Moses was a lawgiver as well as a liberator. Most scholars think he lived in the 13th century B.C. His laws are amazing, far more humane than any other law codes that we know of from that period. Moses had a passion for justice and a desire to protect the defenceless. His laws give protection to slaves - especially women slaves - foreigners, and even animals.

One of his laws shows his concern for oxen, and working animals. People ate a lot of wheat and grain, and they had to remove the tough husk from the grain to be able to use the rich food in the kernel. That was hard to do in those days, without machinery. Often they threshed the wheat by piling it up on a threshing floor and making the oxen walk around and around on it until the husk was ground off.

This could be a tiring and hungry job, especially if the hungry animal could smell the wheat but couldn't eat it. Moses ordered, "You shall not muzzle the mouth of the ox that treads out the grain." The working beast could refresh itself by nibbling through the work day.

Moses' laws provided that animals, as well as humans, had a day of rest once a week. Animals that were killed for food had to be killed humanely. Anyone who came across an animal that was lost and wandering, or that had fallen down under its load, was ordered to stop and help it.

Moses' laws are basic to Jewish ethics. Later Jewish teachers extended and developed these ideas They interpreted Moses' laws to mean that a person should not sit down to eat until the cattle and domestic animals were fed. They also taught that animals should not be docked or mutilated. Ever since Moses, Jewish thinkers have asserted God's love and concern for animals, and the duty of human beings to treat animals kindly. We all owe thanks and respect to this amazing man, who stood for kindness to animals before any other person that we know of.

Isaiah sees a vision of God's peaceable kingdom

8

Isaiah

Isaiah saw a vision of the coming of God's peaceable kingdom, with everything made new and holy.

> The wolf shall dwell with the lamb, and the leopard shall lie down with the kid; and the calf and the young lion and the fatling together; and a little child shall lead them.

> And the cow and the bear shall feed; their young ones shall lie down together; and the lion shall eat straw like the ox.

> They shall not hurt or destroy in all my holy mountain.

Isaiah was a great Jewish prophet, who lived about 600 years after Moses, in the 8th century B.C. He was outstanding in that he saw the coming of God's kingdom as a triumph of love and self-sacrifice, not as a kingdom achieved through the use of power. He was also outstanding in the way he included the animals in the good kingdom to come. He was also concerned for the animals at the present time.

> I delight not in the blood of bulls or of lambs or of goats.

> When you make many prayers I will not hear, your hands are full of blood. Cease to do evil, learn to do good.

Isaiah wrote this at a time when the sacrificing of animals in temples was an almost universal religious practice among the civilized nations of the world.

Mahavira interrupts a sacrifice

Mahavira

In India, early in the 6th century B.C., a religious ceremony was in progress. In a temple enclosure brightly dressed people were gathered. Amid music and flowers, Brahman priests were killing animals in sacrifice.

The ceremony was interrupted by the urgent voice of a wandering preacher. A monk, Mahavira, was talking earnestly about ahimsa. Ahimsa comes from Sanskrit words that mean "not wanting to kill". It has come to mean simply not killing or not harming, or non-violence to living things.

Mahavira spoke eagerly. He tried to persuade the priests not to kill the animals. In the end, he was able to convert three of the Brahman priests to his religion.

Mahavira was the great teacher of a religion called Jainism. It is the Indian religion that has the strongest teachings on non-violence to all living things. One of the teachings of the Jain religion is:

> Whatever beings there are, whether moving or non-moving, you shall not hurt them, knowingly or unknowingly ... for all beings desire to live.

Jains practice "friendship with all beings". They walk carefully to avoid stepping on small creatures. They eat no meat. They are prohibited from trading in ivory, poisons, or weapons. In ancient times, when there was slavery in India, they were prohibited from trading in slaves. They are not allowed to beat, brand, or mutilate animals, to overwork them or to give them inadequate food or water.

Jains filter their water before they drink it, to avoid harming any tiny creatures. Some wear cotton face masks to avoid harming small creatures as they breathe.

Jainism has had a humanizing influence all through history.

In the sixteenth century, a Jain named Hiravijaya Suri had a lot of influence over the Emperor of India, Akbar (who was not a Jain). He persuaded him to release both human prisoners and caged birds. He even persuaded him to give up hunting, which he had greatly enjoyed.

Jains have been leaders in building the thousands of pinjrapoles (animal shelters) all over India.

A French traveller, Rousselot, visited one in 1875. He saw sick cattle lying comfortably on straw, while people rubbed them down. Some animals were blind or paralyzed, so people carried their food to them. There were crows and vultures, blind ducks, and a heron walking on a wooden leg. There were mice, peacocks, jackals, and some remarkably tame rats.

A Jain nun feeds rats in a pinjrapole

Many pinjrapoles have special rooms or cellars to shelter insects. People throw grain in for them.

Some pinjrapoles have a "kutti-ki-roti" (bread for the dog) fund, which provides a daily meal of roti (flat bread) for the wild dogs around the town.

One pinjrapole had a snake-catcher (brave man) who would go to the help of any householder who had a poisonous snake in the house. The snake catcher would catch the snake alive, and take it out in the uninhabited forest and set it free.

In Old Delhi, at the present time, there is a Jain hospital for birds. Anyone can bring in a bird that needs care. There is a veterinarian there to treat the birds. They are fed and cared for, and set free when they recover.

Over the door of each pinjrapole there is a painted sign which says, "Ahimsa paramo dharma" (Ahimsa is the greatest law).

In the 1970's the Jains celebrated the 2500th anniversary of Mahavira's death by leading a movement to ban animal sacrifices in India. They were successful in almost every one of India's states. The state of Gujerat, which has a large population of Jains, also banned hunting for the anniversary year.

Buddha rescues a wounded swan

Buddha

Siddhartha Gautama was the child of a noble family in India. He was born in 563 B.C., about 40 years after Mahavira.

He grew up in a luxurious palace full of beauty and pleasure. He was protected from any knowledge of grief or pain.

One day his cousin, Devadatta, shot a swan. The wounded bird fell in the garden near Gautama. He picked it up and soothed it. Then he drew out the arrow, bandaged it, and cared for it until it was healed.

Devadatta found out where the swan was. He came to Siddhartha and claimed that it was his, because he had shot it. Siddhartha refused to hand it over, saying that it was truly his, because he had healed it.

Siddhartha lived a joyful life as a child and young man. He married and had a baby son.

But then he became aware of the suffering and evil in the world. He decided to leave his home and go out into the world as a wandering monk, begging for his food. He wanted to find a way to free living beings from suffering.

He joined five men who lived in the jungle. They were trying to find wisdom and salvation by living very hard lives. They deprived themselves of every comfort. They never had enough food or sleep. Buddha followed their plan, and was even more extreme than they were. He ate so little that all his bones showed. He had made himself very weak by the time he decided that undergoing extreme bodily suffering was not the answer. He began to eat moderately again.

Then one day, sitting under a tree, he became enlightened. (His title, Buddha, means "enlightened one"). He saw that living in the world, giving in to every desire, was not the way. Living in the forest and denying all the desires of the body was not the way. He had found the right way, the middle path, to satisfy the needs of the body, and keep it in health, without being ruled by desires and attachments. He set out to teach others.

He taught the noble truths about suffering – that suffering is everywhere in the world, and that it is caused by selfish attachment to one's own desires. He showed people the eight-fold path to a good life and freedom from suffering.

People needed eight things for a good life: right views, right aspirations (an intention to lead a life of self discipline and compassion for all beings), right speech, right behavior (no killing, hurting, stealing, lying, or using drugs or alcohol), right livelihood (making a living in a righteous way, not, for example, as a hunter or butcher), right effort, right thought, and right contemplation.

People were drawn to Buddha and his teaching, and he soon had thousands of followers. Some left their homes and became monks and nuns. Others stayed at home with their families and followed the Buddhist precepts, or laws, as lay people.

Buddha's cousin, Devadatta, was jealous of his fame and success. Once when he knew that Buddha was going to walk down a certain path, he ordered the keepers to bring out a fierce and aggressive elephant, and to release it just as Buddha came in sight. Some monks found out what was going to happen, and warned Buddha to go another way, but he went down the path without fear. The maddened elephant charged, and raised its trunk to strike.

Buddha stood still and regarded the elephant with love. It lowered its trunk and stopped the attack, and became quiet and gentle through the power of Buddha's love.

Buddha taught love and compassion for all creatures. His teachings spread rapidly through India, Ceylon, southeast Asia, Tibet, China, Korea and Japan. And wherever Buddhism went, it carried the idea of compassion for living things.

Asoka remembers his conquests with remorse

18

Asoka

A bloody and ruthless conqueror or a gentle Buddhist Emperor - which was Asoka?

Asoka was the grandson of Chandraguptra, a violent and ruthless tyrant. Chandraguptra lived in the small kingdom of Magadha in northeast India. He killed the king of Magadha and all his family and took over the government. He built a huge army and conquered most of India, along with Afghanistan and the nearby areas. He had 600,000 foot soldiers, 30,000 horsemen and 9,000 elephants in his army.

After Chandraguptra and his son, Bindusara, died, Asoka overcame his brothers and seized the throne. He appeared to be following in Chandraguptra's footsteps.

In the eighth year of his reign, around 261 B.C., Asoka invaded the kingdom of the Kalingas, a civilized Indian people. He conquered them, and in doing so he saw a great war, at first hand, with all its death and suffering.

Asoka had many edicts carved on rocks and stone pillars all over India. In one of these, he tells how, right after he conquered the Kalingas, he began to study and love the dharma (the Buddhist law).

He tells of his grief and remorse over the slaughter and enslaving of the Kalinga people - 100,000 killed, 150,000 carried away as captives. He speaks of his regret that the people of Kalinga, Brahmans, holy men of various religions, and ordinary householders, suffered violence and separation from their loved ones.

Asoka says that in the future his conquests will be of a different kind, through the teaching of the Buddhist law. And he urges his sons and grandsons who will come after him to practice patience and gentleness, and not to conquer people by armed force.

Asoka did not attack or conquer any other kingdoms after this. He lived in peace with his neighbors, including many small kingdoms he could easily have conquered.

Up to this time, Asoka had followed the traditional religion, sacrificing animals, eating meat, and leading the royal hunt, the great sport and enjoyment of the emperor and his followers.

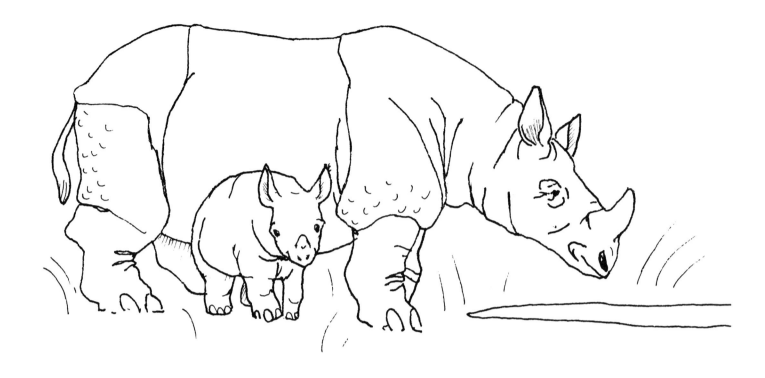

Asoka's rock edicts tell of his changing views. Formerly, he says, thousands of living creatures were slaughtered daily in my kitchens, in the future none will be. He stopped the royal hunt. Instead of "tours of pleasure" (hunting trips) he now took his followers on "tours of dharma" (visits to holy men and elders).

Asoka became an unusually humane emperor. He regarded all human beings as his children, and said he desired their happiness and prosperity, in this world and the next. He urged people to be generous to those in need, and to wandering holy men of all religions. He urged his people to respect other people's religions and not to criticize them. He wanted his people to live simply, to spend little, and not to try to accumulate a lot of wealth.

But what makes Asoka really unique among the great conquerors of the world is the great lengths that he went to for the protection of animals.

In one of his rock edicts, Asoka says that he desires that all animate beings shall have security, self-control, peace of mind and joy.

Asoka worked hard to educate people to have compassion on animals, and to refrain from killing or hurting them. He sent missionaries to all the neighboring kingdoms to teach the dharma.

Asoka passed many laws to protect animals. He forbade animal sacrifices in his capita, Pataliputra. He made it illegal to kill many species of animals, including parrots, ducks, geese, bats, turtles, squirrels, monkeys and rhinoceroses. No one was allowed to kill pregnant animals, or animals that were giving milk. He declared many days to be "non-killing days" on which fish could not be caught or animals killed.

Asoka did many good works for both animals and humans. He had wells dug along the roads at regular intervals for the enjoyment of humans and beasts. He planted fruit and shade trees along the roads, and built resting places and hospitals. He imported medicinal plants to benefit both animals and people, and had them planted in India.

Toward the end of his life Asoka had an edict carved on a stone pillar. It said he was satisfied with the progress of his people. He says that people have grown in reverence for parents, teachers, and old people, and in kindly treatment of holy men, poor people, slaves and servants. He says that piety has grown among the people, and that more and more people abstain from killing animals.

Jesus explains God's love for the birds

Jesus

Jesus shared the Jewish belief that all living things are good and valuable in the eyes of God. He spoke of the beauty and goodness of nature.

> Behold the lilies of the field
> They toil not, neither do they spin,
> Yet Solomon in all his glory
> Was not arrayed as one of these.

He said, strongly and clearly, that God cares for the little birds,

> Behold the fowls of the air,
> For they sow not, neither do they reap,
> nor gather into barns,
> Yet your heavenly father feeds them.

Another time he said,

> Are not five sparrows sold for a farthing?
> And not one of them is forgotten before God.

Jesus taught universal love, gentleness, non-violence, and returning good for evil. Above all, he taught mercy, and promised that people who are merciful will receive mercy.

Jesus lived at a time when animals were killed as sacrifices, both in the Jewish religion in which he grew up, and among the surrounding nations. He once quoted, with approval, the text,

> I will have mercy and not sacrifice.

And when he drew his followers together into a religious community, he established for them a different sort of offering - a nonviolent offering of bread and wine, in which no animal's life is taken.

There have been Christians who claimed that God does not value or love the animals, and therefore human beings have no responsibility to treat animals well. But they are disregarding the plain words and example of Jesus.

Plutarch visits his old horses

Plutarch

Plutarch was a world famous writer. He was a Greek who was renowned all through the Roman Empire. He was also the owner of a farm in the little town of Charonea, in Greece. He was born around 47 A.D.

He had horses and dogs, and oxen to pull the ploughs and wagons on his farm.

Out in his pastures, you could see the powerful working beasts - and among them, some old, worn out animals. They had been too old to do any useful work for a long time. Plutarch would never sell them or have them slaughtered, because, he said:

> We must not treat living creatures like old shoes or
> dishes, and throw them away when they are worn out
> or broken with service.

Plutarch is one of the great writers of the world, loved and read over the centuries. Kindness and humanity shine through his pages.

He lived in the days when the Roman Empire ruled the whole Mediterranean area, including Greece. Life was brutal in many ways. Plutarch believed that the role of Greek education was to make the world more humane.

He was concerned about justice and humanity for human beings. And he was unusual in his time and place because he said that animals also deserve justice and humanity.

Other writers said that animals are not intelligent and rational, and therefore they don't have any rights. Plutarch believed the opposite.

He was very interested in animals. He wrote essays about the intelligence of animals. He tells about incidents he has seen or heard of that prove that animals have a lot of intelligence.

He says he saw a dog acting a play. In the play, the dog is supposed to be poisoned. The dog actor did an amazing job of playing the role of a poisoned animal. Plutarch also says he saw a dog on shipboard who wanted to lick the oil out of a half-empty jar. The intelligent dog dropped stones in the jar until the oil rose to a level he could reach with his tongue.

Plutarch says that when an elephant was trapped in a deep pit, the other elephants rolled rocks and dirt down into the pit, until the trapped elephant was able to climb out.

Plutarch also says that he observed a hedgehog carrying grapes to its cub. The hedgehog had solved the problem of carrying a lot of grapes at once by rolling around in the grapes until there were grapes stuck all over its sharp quills, and it looked like a walking bunch of grapes. Plutarch concludes that animals have a lot of intelligence and deserve justice.

Plutarch says that people could recognize the rights of animals and still make a fair use of them, by raising animals to work, and for wool and milk, which can be used without harming the animal.

As a young man, Plutarch wrote two essays against meat eating. He said that meat eating is not natural for human beings. His proof is that humans do not have the claws and sharp canine teeth that meat eating animals have.

Plutarch says that the earth gives us ample food without our having to use meat. But, he says, if anyone feels that they need to eat meat, then, at least, the animals used for meat should be killed humanely.

We will kill an animal, but in pity and sorrow, not abusing or torturing it.

Plutarch is the first of many people in the humane movement to say this.

He disliked hunting because it strengthens the urge to kill, and deadens pity.

Plutarch detested the popular Roman entertainments, the gladiatorial games, in which hundreds of thousands of people, and even more animals, were killed for entertainment. He wanted them stopped.

Plutarch was a great writer, and a great human being. He used his genius to try to bring about a better world.

Rabbi Judah ha-Nasi

Moses laid the foundation, by making a duty to animals a part
of the Jewish religion. After Moses, generations of Rabbis,
saints, scholars and teachers worked out the details. The
histories, legends, and teachings of humane Jews helped build up
a culture that was concerned for animals. The story of Judah
ha-Nasi is a good example.

Judah ha-Nasi was a scholar and teacher in Palestine in the
2nd century. He was also a Prince. The whole Mediterranean
area was under Roman rule. He ruled a large area of Palestine
under the Roman governor. He used his power to protect his
people. One little story has come down to us about Rabbi Judah
and the animals.

Once when he was sitting studying, in front of the synagogue,
a calf came by which was being led to the slaughterhouse. It
seemed to understand the fate that was ahead for it, and it ran
to Rabbi Judah to appeal for rescue. He rebuffed it, saying,
"Go, for you were made for this purpose!" The Talmud says that
God punished him for his heartlessness. He had a toothache for
thirteen years. Then one day a servant was sweeping his house.
She found a nest of little weasels, and was going to sweep them
out. Rabbi Judah stopped her, saying, "Let them be, for His
tender mercies are over all His works". Because he had
compassion on the animals, God had compassion on him and healed
him.

Theon draws water for the desert animals

The Desert Fathers

In the 4th century A.D., many Christian men and women were filled with enthusiasm. They desired to give up everything for God - homes, families, and possessions. Thousands went to live in the deserts of Egypt as nuns, monks, and hermits. They are called the desert fathers.

Many stories are told of their search for a life of total love, and their kindly interaction with both animals and humans. They lived in utter poverty, working as farm laborers or basket makers, living on little, giving most of their small pay to help the needy, saving nothing.

One of these desert fathers was a hermit named Theon. He lived alone for thirty years in a little hut. Every night he walked to a deep water hole to get water, and a troop of desert animals went with him for company. When he drew water from the well for himself, he drew it for the animals also. He offered them cup after cup of water until they had all had enough. Gazelles and wild goats and donkeys flocked around him.

In another part of the desert, a little group of monks had a tame donkey. They lived high up a mountain. At the foot of the mountain was a little vegetable garden, which an old man tended for them. When they ran out of food, they told the donkey to go get them some vegetables. He would go off, all by himself, down the mountain, and the gardener would load him with vegetables. Then he walked back up the mountain to bring the monks their food. He walked up and down the mountain, taking care of the old men, but he would not obey anyone else.

A story is told about a hermit named Poemen. He lived in a cave in a remote part of the desert. Some visitors came to him once, and stayed overnight. His cave was bitterly cold, and they woke up feeling frozen. In the morning, they asked Poemen why he wasn't cold. He told them that a lion had gotten in the habit of coming into his cave every night, and sleeping beside him, and the warmth of the lion's great furry body kept him warm all night.

Sometimes it was the animals who helped the hermits, as in this story. A man went to live in the desert as a hermit. He planned to live on the desert plants and roots. He became very sick, because all the plants tasted good, but many wild plants are poisonous. He had no way of knowing which plants were good to eat. He was having horrible stomach pains, and felt close to death, when an ibex, a wild goat, came up to him. He tossed it a bunch of the plants he had collected. The ibex used its nose to shove the poisonous plants aside and separate out the safe ones. Thus the hermit learned which plants he could eat, and he recovered.

Another old man lived alone in a tiny hut. Every evening at dinner time a she-wolf came to him, and he gave her any bread that he had left from his dinner. The wolf ate it, politely licked his hand, and went on her way.

One day the old man had visitors, and when they left he went with them and walked part of the way home with them. The she-wolf came at dinner time, but he wasn't home. She went in the hut, saw a hanging basket of bread, and took a whole loaf of bread and ate it.

The old man came home and found his bread supply raided!

The wolf apparently felt guilty, for she did not return for seven days. The old man missed his companion, and prayed for her to come back.

She came back, looking guilty and embarassed. The hermit stroked her head and fed her a double ration of bread. That cheered her up, and she went back to making her regular evening visits, to the delight of the hermit.

Saint Martin stops the hounds and saves a hare

Saint Martin of Tours

Martin was a young soldier in the Roman army. He lived in the province called Gaul (the part of Europe which is France now). It was around 330 A.D. His kindly nature showed, even then, when he was a teen-aged soldier.

The country was in turmoil. Armies of barbarians were invading, and there were many refugees and poor people. One cold winter, Martin had given away all his spare clothes to the swarms of desperate people. He had nothing left but the clothes he was wearing. A poor shivering man begged Martin for something warm to wear. Martin drew his sword and cut his great woolly soldier's cloak in half, and gave half to the man. That way they both were fairly well protected against the bitter cold.

Martin left the army, entered the church, and soon became a bishop in Gaul. When people gave money to the church, he would not let the church keep anything more than the necessary operating expenses. He insisted that any money beyond that bare minimum must be used to help people in need. He used church funds to ransom people who had been captured by the barbarians. If they were not ransomed, they would be sold as slaves.

Sometimes there were disputes over doctrines in the church. One group of people would say that others, who disagreed with them, were "heretics". Then they would try to persuade the Emperor to execute the "heretics". Martin used his influence to try to stop the Emperor from executing them.

Martin had a gift for healing mentally ill people, and was able to help many of them. He found that his gift also worked with disturbed animals. Once he was able to heal a mentally ill patient - a cow - which had gone crazy and was attacking people with her horns.

Martin had to travel around the country a lot, doing his work as a bishop. Once when he was travelling, he met a band of hunters. They were chasing a hare with their dogs. The poor hare was exhausted and could not run much more. It was just about to be caught. As it zigzagged past him, Martin stepped into the path of the dogs and roared a command to stop. The dogs stopped in their tracks as if frozen, and the little hare escaped.

Telemachus throws himself into the amphitheater

Telemachus

It was the year 404 A.D. 45,000 people sat in the bleachers of the Colosseum, the great amphitheater at Rome, to watch the gladiatorial show.

Men were to fight to the death, animals were to fight to the death, men were to kill animals, animals were to kill people.

No one paid any attention to the man from Syria. Yet it was strange to see a man in a Christian hermit's robe at the games, for the church taught that going to see those bloody shows was totally against the Christian religion.

The man in the hermit's robe walked on, down the steps, closer and closer to the arena, up to the barricades that separated the audience from the fighters.

Two men were fighting furiously. It looked as though the end was near for one of them.

Then Telemachus, the gentle, idealistic hermit, was over the barricade. He thrust himself between the astonished gladiators. Now he was shouting, his voice could be heard in the sudden silence. He was shouting to the men not to kill each other, shouting to the crowd, begging for an end to the cruelty and killing. The silence lasted long enough for the crowd to grasp his message.

They responded with fury. They were excited, stirred up by watching the fighting, they wanted to see more, they wanted to see the deaths. They were angry at the interruption, and angry at Telemachus' messsage.

The crowd grabbed everything hard and heavy that they could find. They tore up stones and railings, and threw them down on Telemachus with all their strength. Telemachus, still standing, separating the gladiators, was quickly struck down and killed.

The news was sent to the Emperor, Honorius. Honorius was a Christian and he disapproved of the games. Three years earlier, he had closed the gladiatorial schools where men were trained to kill. But he had not felt able to stop the games. The turbulent Roman mob demanded them, and would riot if they they didn't get them.

The murder of Telemachus, who was well-known as a holy man, made Honorius angry. He made a strong decision. There would be no more killing of human beings for entertainment. He decreed the permanent closing of the gladiatorial games.

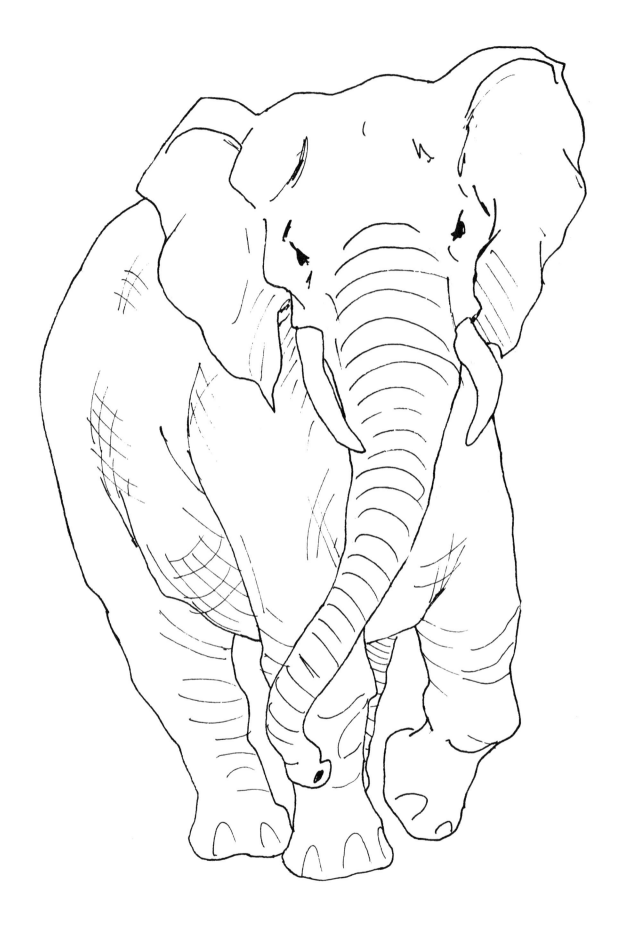

Stopping the animal games saved thousands of elephants from a
barbarous death

It was a long job, the fight to end the human and animal games in the arena.

Plutarch and a few other Greek and Roman writers opposed them. The Jewish community was totally against them. The writers of the early Christian church denounced them.

Constantine, the first Christian Emperor, managed to get them stopped in some cities in the Greek part of the Empire. He had horse races instead.

After Telemachus' self-sacrifice, Honorius stopped the killing of human beings in the arena, but the killing of animals continued for another hundred years.

The Christian writer, Cassiodorus, said that the animal-killing games had been brought to Rome as a part of the worship of pagan goddesses, and that whoever invented those games was fit to rule in hell. He lived long enough to see the end of them, in 523 A.D. After that, the amphitheaters were neglected and disused, and people quarried their stones to use for building.

The man who did the most for this cause was Telemachus, who made the long journey from Syria to Rome, and went into the hated arena, and gave his life to stop those evil shows.

...and bears, too!

"I will die sooner than make them suffer"

Fan's Wife and other Taoists

The wife of a Chinese soldier named Fan was very sick.   She had tuberculosis. Very few people recovered from it in those days. Her doctors told her that she would be cured if she ate the brains of a hundred sparrows.

A cage was brought to her house. She stood looking at the lively little birds. Suddenly she knew that she did not want to save her life at the cost of the bird's lives. She opened the cage and freed the birds, saying,

"I will die sooner than make them suffer".

But afterwards she recovered her health.

The story of Fan's wife is among the moral tales which are attached to some editions of the "Kan-ying p'ien". It is a Chinese Taoist book of moral principles and stories.   It was written in China sometime in the middle ages. It has been immensely popular for many centuries. Millions of copies of it have been made.

Taoism, the religion that produced the Kan-ying p'ien, is an ancient Chinese religion.   Its first great teacher, Lao Tzu, lived in the 6th century B.C. His teachings are set forth in a great book, the Tao Te Ching.

Lao Tzu wanted everyone to cooperate with the great creative force in the universe, which he called Tao, the Way. He said,

> The highest good is like water
> It benefits the ten thousand creatures.
> It does not strive, but is content
> With the low places men disdain.
> And this makes water like the Tao.

Lao Tzu praised "the valley spirit, the mother, the female". He rejected violence - "Where Tao is present, the horses work at peaceful tasks" (instead of war).   He disliked even beautiful weapons, and praised the wise men who preserve life, who care for all men, who care for all creatures.

Two great followers of Lao Tzu, Lieh Yu-kou and Chuang Tzu, lived two centuries later.   Lieh lived a little earlier than Chuang. He was teaching around 398 B.C.

Lieh Yu-kou saw the likeness between humans and animals.   He asked,

"How are the minds of birds and beasts different from the minds of men?"   He said that the shapes and sounds are different, so we can't communicate, but that animals are like

An old man carries fodder to the "given-up-cows"

us in many ways - in innate intelligence, desiring to live, loving their mates, and caring for their young.

He believed that in an early, golden age, animals did not fear humans, but kept company with them, and only later began to fear and avoid them.

Lieh tells of a banquet where the host was praising God for giving people all the living creatures to eat. A twelve year old boy of the Pao family was moved to speak up and answer. He said that all species are equal, and not made for food for each other. Sometimes one kind of living thing, by strength or cunning, catches and eats another, but this does not mean God ordered it so. We do not believe that God made humans to be food for mosquitoes or wolves or tigers, although they feed on us at times, the boy said.

Chuang Tzu praised Lieh's work. He also praised Lao Tzu for teaching non-injury to living things.

The next great philosopher of the Taoist school was Ko Hung. He lived around 284-364 A.D. He wrote under a pen-name, Pao-p'u Tzu (the sage who clings to simplicity). He taught that the universe is ruled by a merit system, and that those who want immortality must earn it by good works. Their hearts must be kind to all things, and they must treat others like themselves and be humane even to insects. They must pity the suffering and save the poor. Their hands must never injure life.

He told people to avoid stealing, lying, gossip, bribe-taking, injustice, and massacring prisoners. His teaching helped to solidify Taoism into an organized system.

Taoists have run animal shelters, like the pinjrapoles of India, sometimes in their temples, sometimes as private citizens. In the late 19th century, travellers told of an old Chinese man (name unknown) who bought old, worn-out cows and kept them in his shelter, the "Office for Given-Up Cows". He later added a dog tent to shelter needy dogs. This man was very likely a Taoist or a follower of the I-Kuan Tao (way of unity) which blends the teachings of Lao Tzu, Buddha, and Confucius. Taoist and Buddhist teachings of compassion are very strong in this system, as the following quotations show:

> People who wish to follow the Way must practice compassion.
> An insect or bird has, like us, a heavenly nature.
> Human beings have a short life and must not be enemies to animals.

Emperor Wu-Ti insists on dough animals for sacrifice

The Emperors Wu-Ti and Yuan

In 502 A.D. a Chinese prince named Hsaio-Yen became the first Emperor of the Liang dynasty. His name as Emperor was Wu-Ti. He was a serious, thoughtful young man. In his youth, he was a Taoist, a follower of the contemplative and non-violent religion founded by Lao Tzu. He had many friends among Chinese Buddhist monks. He was impressed by their good lives, and he became a convert to Buddhism.

In 511, he stopped the use of meat in the palace kitchens. In 517 he forbade the use of living things in religious sacrifices. He commanded that people should make offerings of fruits and vegetables, or else make sacrificial animals out of dough.

The Emperor sometimes put on a Buddhist monk's robe and did menial work in a temple for a few days. He was compassionate toward criminals, and disliked punishing or executing people.

The Emperor Yuan of the same dynasty began to rule in 552. He was also greatly impressed by Buddhist teachings. He especially believed in the duty to help and rescue living beings. He built a pavilion with a fresh water pond in it. This pond is the first one recorded in history of the famous "fang-sheng chih" (ponds for releasing life). They were usually built by devout Buddhists. People bought shrimp, fish, turtles and other small water animals from the food merchants, saved them from being killed and eaten, and released them in the ponds.

The practice of building these ponds and releasing living creatures in them became enormously popular in China. The T'ang dynasty Emperor Su-tsung in 759 ordered the building of eighty-one such ponds.

Mohammed saves a camel from death by thirst

Mohammed

Arabia in the 6th century A.D. was a rough place. There was slavery, constant tribal wars, cruelty to humans and animals.

When a man died, in accordance with a widespread custom, his camel was tethered to a stake beside his grave and left there, until it died of hunger and thirst.

Mohammed, the teacher of a new religion, could not stand this practice. It was hard to get people to stop, but he was absolutely determined. As his followers increased in number, and gained power over more and more of Arabia, the custom was stamped out.

Mohammed taught the idol-worshipping Arabians a new religion, a faith in one God, the merciful, the compassionate. Mohammed liked animals, and believed that they also had a share in God's love. He believed that they would share with humans in the resurrection after death. He said,

> There is no earthly beast or winged bird that is not a people like mankind, and they shall return to the Lord.

Mohammed made many practical rules to protect animals:

> Fear God with the dumb animals - ride them when they are fit for it, and get off them when they are tired.

He would not allow anyone to clip the manes or tails of horses, because they need them to protect themselves from biting flies. If he saw men overloading donkeys or horses he had them arrested.

He told a story about a woman who had committed many sins. One day she saw a dog dying of thirst. She had no rope or bucket to draw water from the well, but she took off her shoe, and using her belt as a rope, drew up water and saved the dog. Mohammed said that because of her kindness, all her sins were forgiven, for,

> There are rewards for doing good to the four-footed beasts and giving them water. There are rewards for doing good to all the kinds of living creatures.

45

Rabi'a al Adawiyya

In Basra, in what is now Iraq, a baby girl was born in 717. Her family was very poor, and already had three daughters. On the night she was born, her family had neither oil for the lamp, nor clothes for the baby. That night the father was comforted when the Prophet Mohammed appeared to him in a dream, and said, "Do not be sorrowful, for this daughter who is born is a great saint."

Worse troubles followed. The parents died, and there was a great famine. Rabi'a was somehow separated from her sisters. An evil man kidnapped her and sold her as a slave.

Rabi'a was a Sufi in religion. She belonged to a Islamic school that teaches that the goal of life is total love of God, and total union with him.

Yet she was a slave. She had nothing, not even her freedom. Who could believe that some day she would be a revered spiritual teacher in Islam?

Rabi'a worked hard all day. At night she denied herself sleep so that she could pray and meditate and draw close to God. One night the slaveowner looked out his window. He saw Rabi'a standing, surrounded by radiance. She was saying,

> O my Lord, you know that my heart desires to obey you, and the light of my eyes is serving you, but I am under a human master.

The slaveholder sat until dawn, thinking about this. Then he called Rabi'a to him, talked to her kindly, and set her free.

Rabi'a went to the desert for a time to meditate and pray. Then she returned to Basra, where she lived in simplicity and poverty. She refused gifts of money and riches. She also refused many offers of marriage. She used to go up on the roof at night and pray,

> O my Lord, bright are the stars, men's eyes are closed, each lover is alone with the beloved, and I am here, alone with Thee.

Many stories are told of her poor and simple life, of her giving her bread to beggars, and her tireless teaching, free, the many women and men who came to her.

Her kindness included the animals. When she was in the mountains, the animals came to her, deer, gazelle, mountain goats and wild donkeys. They gathered around her, trusting and fearless. When a friend, another religious teacher named Hasan-al-Basri, came up to her, the animals ran away.

He asked why the animals were friendly with her, but fled from him. She asked what he had eaten. He said, "Onions fried in fat". She said, "If you eat their fat, of course they will flee from you".

Rabi'a was an amazingly gifted woman, a mystic, a teacher, a poet. Her life was a struggle to abandon all earthly things and focus on God alone - yet she could spare attention and kindness for the wild animals of the desert.

The   Empress   Jito

Women had a lot of freedom and authority in Japan in the
early middle ages.   In the 7th and 8th centuries the Mikado
(Supreme Ruler) of Japan was often a woman.

Many of these women were Buddhists, and used their authority
to encourage reverence for life. The Empress Jito, the 41st
Mikado, was one of these. She ruled from 686 to 697 A.D.

She encouraged people to become Buddhist monks or nuns, built
temples and had copies made of Buddhist scriptures. She ordered
the teaching of Buddhism in various provinces.

She did not forget the animals. She encouraged "hojo" (the
releasing of captive animals), and set up "long life places"
(refuges where animals could not be hunted), both in the capital
and out in the provinces.

By the time of the Empress Jito, Buddhism had been growing in Japan for over a hundred years.

Buddhism first came to Japan from Korea. It was probably in the year 538 that Seimeio, the King of Kudara in southwest Korea, sent some gifts to the Emperor of Japan. He sent copies of Buddhist scriptures, a statue of Buddha, and a letter praising the goodness of the Buddhist law.

The Emperor, Kimmei, was delighted with the gifts. He admired the beauty of the teachings, and the serene and radiant face of the statue. A few years later he made a law against cruel funeral rites. He forbade his people to sacrifice horses or human beings at funerals. Scholars think this law was the result of Buddhist teachings.

Kimmei's daughter Suiko was the first woman Mikado. She named her 19 year old nephew, Prince Shotoku, Crown Prince and Regent. Suiko and Shotoku encouraged and supported Buddhism, and ruled in accordance with the precepts of Buddhism. They provided for the care of orphans and sick people, passed laws to protect animals, and built Buddhist schools and temples. They sent scholars to China to bring back Buddhist books and translate them. In 604, Prince Shotoku wrote a constitution. It favored harmony and regard for public opinion, and warned officials against tyranny.

After Shotoku's death the violent Soga clan attacked his son and family. The family could have beaten them, but they chose instead to follow Buddha's teachings of non-violence, rather than starting a civil war. They were all killed, unresisting. The Soga rule only lasted two years. Then power returned to the Mikado's family.

A little later, another Buddhist ruler, the Emperor Temmu, in 675, forbade the eating of various animals, including cattle, horses, dogs and monkeys. His niece, who followed him as the 41st Mikado, was the Empress Jito described above.

The Empress Ko-ken, the 46th Mikado, in 754 welcomed a group of Chinese Buddhist teachers who came to share their learning and religion with the Japanese. She was deeply moved at the selflessness of these men and women who risked their lives through pirates and typhoons to come to Japan. One monk in this group was Hosshin, who was especially concerned with reverence for the lives of sentient beings. The Empress Ko-ken, after the arrival of these teachers, received the Buddhist precepts in a formal public ceremony. She left much of the work of government to her ministers, but she was personally responsible for some of the laws to protect animals.

Abu l'Ala

Share thy water with the early birds,
    For this is a worthwhile deed,
The birds do no harm nor sin,
    But beware and fear thy kind.

Freeing an insect is kinder
    Than giving money to the needy,
There is no difference between releasing
    The deformed black creature,
And the black prince of Kinda,
    Ready to be crowned.
Both deserve living, for their lives are precious,
And seeking to live is a continual struggle.

So said Abu l'Ala, the blind poet. He was born at Ma'arrat
in Syria, in 973, more than three hundred years after Mohammed.
When he was three, he caught smallpox, which left him almost
totally blind.

Ma'arrat was a town full of poets and scholars.   The whole
Arab world at that time was having an explosion of learning,
poetry and science.   Many historians, poets, theologians,
scientists and doctors were writing books, and many Arab towns
had extensive libraries.

Abu l'Ala was eager to learn, in spite of his blindness.
With the help of good teachers and his amazing memory, he soon
mastered much of Arabic literature. In his teens, he travelled
to all the towns of Syria that had good libraries, and learned
many of the books by heart. In 993 he returned to Ma'arrat,
where he lived on a small pension and began to write poetry. In

Abu l'Ala can't bear it when animals are beaten

1008 he went to Bagdad, the great capital, and joined in discussions with the great thinkers of the day. He learned a lot, and thought deeply. In 1010 he returned to Ma'arrat, where he planned to live a solitary, ascetic, vegetarian life. But he was becoming famous, and disciples and students came to him. He was not alone, but was surrounded by people who wanted to learn from him.

He lived well as a professional poet and teacher. Because of his blindness, friends wrote down his poetry for him.

Abu l'Ala was a genius with words, he could move and persuade people. He used his power for justice and the defence of the oppressed.

Soon he had his first chance to try to help other people by his eloquence. Some of his fellow townsmen rioted and wrecked a tavern. The angry governor, Salih, put seventy citizens in jail. Abu l'Ala made a moving speech to the governor and persuaded him to release all seventy of them.

Abu l'Ala wrote poetry to try to improve people's ideas. He spoke out for religious equality, and urged Jews, Christians, and Moslems to respect one another's religions and behave with good will toward each other. He denounced polygamy because it is hard on women. He denounced bad rulers, and said that rulers and princes are the servants of the people. He hated war and said that kings who made war would burn in hell.

Over and over, he used his poetry to urge compassion for animals:

> My heart bleeds for the cruelty toward
> The poor burro, who stubbornly endures,
> But also gets whipped for resting because of
> The excessive burden on his back.

He was a vegetarian because he did not want to hurt animals.

> Neither eat the sea creatures,
> For this is cruel,
> Nor seek or desire thy food
> From the painful slaughtering of animals.

He went so far as to object to the use of fur, leather, honey, milk, and eggs, because they involve taking something from animals.

Abu l'Ala Ahmad ibn 'Abdallah al-Ma'arri was learned in Arabic literature and knew the commandments of Mohammed about mercy to animals. He carried the idea even further, and used his gift of poetry to promote mercy to both humans and animals.

Buddhist monks and nuns of Japan

After Buddhism came to Japan, thousands of men and women became monks or nuns. Many went abroad to study with Buddist teachers. Zenshinni, for example, was a Japanese nun. She went with a group of nuns to study in Korea. They returned to Japan in 590. Buddhist teachers from China and even India came to Japan. One of these was Hosshin, the man from China who was welcomed by the Empress Ko-ken. He taught people to set animals free, and not eat them. He taught that even "mote creatures" (very tiny organisms) have the Buddha nature.

Many beautiful stories are told of the works of kindness that were done by the Buddhists of Japan.

Dosho was a monk who studied in China, and came back to Japan in 661. He practiced meditation, and also did many works of kindness to help people, such as digging wells and building bridges. His student, Gyogi, travelled all over Japan. He built bridges and schools and planted fruit trees as he travelled.

Kukai was another monk who studied in China. He returned in 806. He was famous for building reservoirs for water, and building schools for poor boys.

Eisai was a monk who founded zen Buddhism in Japan. Once he was working with a sheet of copper, which was very expensive, to make a halo for a statue of Buddha. A poor man came to the door to beg for help for his hungry family. Instantly, Eisai crumpled up the copper halo and gave it to the man. He told him that he could sell it and get enough money to buy food for his family for a long time.

The other monks criticized Eisai for giving away the Buddha's halo. Eisai reminded them that Buddha had come into the world to give himself for all beings, and that his followers had a duty to keep people from starving.

His disciple, Eizon, was born in 1201. He travelled all over Japan. He had a special care for the "Hinin", the outcast untouchable people of Japan. They were very poor. There were many lepers among them. He gave them money and rice, and worked among them, repairing their houses. He taught them the Buddhist law. In a bad famine in 1268, he was able to raise money and feed over 50,000 people.

Eizon's most famous disciple, Ryonkanbo Ninsho, became a vegetarian at age 13. Like Eizon, he was active in caring for anyone in need. He and his disciples built and operated hospitals and orphan homes, and refuges for beggars. In 1298 he built a hospital for horses.

Ryokan, a monk who lived much later, around 1800, loved animals and loved to share his food with birds and little animals. He once tore the floor and roof out of his little hut to allow a bamboo shoot to grow. He wandered around the countryside, and enjoyed the company of beggars and robbers. He loved to play with children, and they loved him, and would shout with delight when he showed up in their villages. Ryonkan went to the extreme of letting mosquitoes bite his legs, and carrying lice around in his pockets.

These are only a few of the many people who worked vigorously to care for living beings in Japan. We don't even know the names of most of them. Their work was on a large scale, and helped many people. In just one of Ninsho's hospitals, the one in Kuwadani, about 80 percent of the patients were helped. In the space of 20 years, 46,800 people were sent home cured from that hospital.

Saint Francis

A little, thin man, poorly dressed in rough brown cloth, used to pick up worms when he found them in the middle of the road, and put them on the side in safety.

One day he came out of his cell and saw a cicada near him on a branch. He held out a hand to it, and said, "Come to me, my sister cicada!" The cicada jumped on his hand, and he stroked it, saying, "Sing, my sister cicada!" The cicada began to chirp, and Saint Francis joyfully praised God along with it. They went on doing this for an hour, and then he put it back on the branch. For the next eight days, Francis always found her waiting on the branch, and she jumped on his hand and sang for him. Saint Francis' love of living things was so great that many wild creatures were friendly in his presence.

Saint Francis was a young man of Assisi. He chose to live in deep poverty., begging his bread. He delighted to live among the poor, serving them and preaching to them. He cared for lepers and other sick people, and welcomed robbers and outcasts. As other men and women were inspired to join him, he became the founder of the Franciscan order of friars. His friend, Saint Clare, joined him and founded the women's order called the Poor Clares.

Saint Francis rejoiced in the beauty of the world, and wrote poetry praising Brother Sun, Sister Moon, Brother Fire and Sister Water. Even more, he loved our brothers and sisters the living creatures. He taught that everyone should be generous to animals and birds.

Saint Frances makes an agreement with a wolf

Once when he was travelling, he came to some trees, filled with innumerable birds. Full of love and joy, he left his companions and walked among the trees to preach to "our sisters, the birds". He spoke to them of God's great love and care for them. He asked them to praise God, and the birds responded with loud singing.

Francis brought honey to the bees, to help them through a hard winter. He was seen throwing freshly-caught fish back in the water. One day, in Ancona, he gave his cloak to a butcher, in exchange for two lambs, to save them from slaughter. He urged people to throw out grain for the birds to eat. He was loved and followed by many pet animals - lambs, rabbits and pheasants.

Once he arrived at the town of Gubbio, and heard that a huge and ferocious wolf was terrorizing the town. It attacked and killed both animals and people. The people were afraid to walk outside the town.

Francis set out to find the wolf, while the people watched from their roofs.

The wolf appeared, and charged toward Francis. He spoke to it, and it stopped. "Brother Wolf", he said, "I want you to stop being wicked." He asked the wolf to make peace with the people of the town, and to do no more killing. In return, the people would feed the wolf, and neither they nor their dogs would do him any harm.

The wolf put his paw in Francis' hand and agreed, and the townspeople swore to take care of the wolf. For the rest of his life, the wolf came and went freely and peacefully through the town, the people fed him, and their dogs did not even bark at him.

Saint Bonaventure was a scholar and theologian. He joined the Franciscan order in 1243, 17 years after Francis' death. He wrote a biography of Saint Francis. In it, he tells how Saint Francis called all the living creatures, no matter how small, by the name of brother or sister, because they came from the same source as himself.

Saint Bonaventure developed this idea in his writings on theology. He believed that all creatures come from God and return to God. He said that the light of God shines through the different creatures in different ways. He told people to see, hear, praise and love God in all creatures.

Rabbi Weil forbids the blessing of a fur coat

Rabbi Weil and Rabbi Meir

Jews say a lot of blessings in their daily lives. They say blessings over meals and at many other times. One common blessing is said when a person puts on a new piece of clothing for the first time. Someone asked a medieval Rabbi, Rabbi Weil, if it was permissible to say a blessing over a new fur coat. He said no. He reasoning was this: the customary blessing says, may you outlive this coat and put on another one. Saying that blessing would imply that the killing of fur bearing animals to make the coat was a good thing. That would contradict the verse, "His tender mercies are over all His works".

People asked rabbis many questions like this, about matters of right and wrong. Rabbis wrote their answers ("Responsa"). These Responsa were read and studied by scholars near and far. Many of these Responsa are about people's obligations to animals. They add up to a body of laws that protect animals in many ways.

The great scholar Moses Maimonides, who lived in the 12th century, said that it is prohibited in Biblical law to cause pain to an animal. He said that "we must not kill out of cruelty or for sport." He said that Jewish slaugtering regulations were carefully designed to bring about the most painless possible death for the animal.

Rabbi Meir ben Baruch of Rothenburg (1215-1293) was one of the greatest scholars of the Middle Ages. Students came to him from all over Germany. People sent questions for his judgement from as far away as Spain.

He wrote many Responsa about law and government, always defending human freedom and government by consent of the governed. When the Emperor Rudolph I tried to declare the Jews of Germany to be serfs of the Imperial Treasury (so he could lay extra taxes on them) Rabbi Meir, outraged, organized a mass exodus from the area. He was caught and imprisoned. The Jewish community was willing to pay a huge ransom for his release, but the Emperor would only release him if he and the community agreed that they were serfs. They would not agree, so Rabbi Meir died in prison.

Hunting was a popular sport, and sometimes people asked Rabbi Meir if it was allowable to enjoy hunting. His answer was strong. He said that any Jew who went hunting would be denied life in the world to come. This position was repeated in the Responsa of many later Rabbis.

While most Jews eat meat, but insist on humane farming and slaughter, there are also quite a few Jews who are vegetarians. The great mystic Isaac Luria was one of these. He is commonly known as "The Ari". He lived first in Egypt and then at Safed in Palestine in the 16th Century. He was a great scholar and teacher and had many followers. He taught them never to kill or cause pain to a living creature, not even a worm or an insect. Rabbi Luria and his followers were members of the mystical Kabballist movement and were vegetarians.

Jewish authors have pointed out that in the account of the Creation in Genesis, human beings, before they disobeyed God and became sinful, are pictured as vegetarians, at peace with all the animals.

Saint Sergius of Rostov

In winter the Russian forests are bitterly cold, and the forest animals are often hungry.

A young monk lived in a cell near a river in a forest north of Moscow, at a place called Makovitsa. He had a little garden, grew vegetables, and ground his own wheat. Sometimes visitors came and brought him a little food, but his food sometimes ran short, especially in winter.

Every day a bear came to his hut. It was not hostile, but seemed to be looking for something to eat. Sergius brought out a loaf of bread for the bear. Some days he had no bread, and he and the bear both went hungry. Sometimes he had only one small piece of bread, and then he would give it to the bear, even though that meant that he himself would go hungry.

This loving act was typical of the humble, self-giving spirit of Saint Sergius.

He was born in 1314 in the Russian city of Rostov. He loved to tend the horses and walk among the woods and lakes of the beautiful Russian countryside. In his teens, he felt a desire to go live as a monk, alone in the forest, but his parents, who were old and sick, wanted him to stay with them. Sergius lovingly cared for them until they died.

When they died, Sergius was twenty years old. He gave up all his property and went to live in the forest. His older brother Stephen came and joined him. The bishop gave them permission to build a chapel. They worked away with ax and saw, and built a chapel and a little cell to live in. Stephen could not stand the cold winters and the lack of food, so he left, and went to live in a monastery in Moscow. Sergius stayed, and three years later, when the Abbot Metrophanes came to visit him, he swore the vows of a monk. He worked in his garden, read the Bible, and tried to grow in love and humility.

Other men were drawn to him, and wanted to come and live at Makovitsa. Sergius could not refuse them. He was young and strong, so he built cells for them with his own hands. They wanted him to be their abbot, but he refused, for he did not want power or authority. He did the hard work, cutting wood, baking bread, making boots and fetching water.

The monks finally, with great difficulty, persuaded him to be their abbot. He continued to do the hard manual work. He ruled his little community so gently, it was said that he was both father and servant to the other monks.

Saint Sergius became very influential. So many people wanted to join him that he founded several other monasteries besides the first one, Trinity Lavra at Makovitsa. Princes and rulers asked his advice. Sergius was able to stop much of the fighting between Russian cities, and to bring about unity and peace. He stood up for the rights of poor peasants when the rich and powerful oppressed them. A community of peasants grew up outside the monastery, because they wanted to live near Saint Sergius.

Saint Sergius caused a wave of enthusiasm and renewal in the Russian Church. His work was very effective, this man who would go hungry in the cold winter to feed a bear.

"Don't kill them!" cried Filippo Neri

Saint Filippo Neri

An old man was lying in his room, feeling ill. Flies were buzzing around. Sometimes one landed on his face or hands. His disciple, Francesco, came running to the rescue, fly swatter in hand.

"Don't kill them!" cried Filippo, the old man, hastily. He gave Francesco his cloak, and asked him to open the window and chase the flies out with the cloak.

All his life long, Filippo Neri protected and rescued living things.

He was born in Florence in 1515, but he went to Rome as a young man. There, in the middle of the great city, he tried to live like the desert fathers.

He sold his books and gave the money to the poor. He worked without pay, tending the poor and sick in the city hospital of Rome. The patients said he treated them like "Gran Signnori" (great lords). He begged for his bread and gave to others whatever he had.

Filippo had a deep feeling for animals. He could not stand to see them suffer. When mice were caught in traps, he carried them away from people's houses and released them in fields and stables. He could not bear to pass a butcher's shop. "Ah", he cried, "if everyone were like me (he was a vegetarian) no one would kill animals!"

In Filippo's time, misguided churchmen persecuted those whose beliefs were different from their own, both Jews and their fellow Christians. Filippo hated this cruelty, and sometimes succeeded in saving people from execution.

He was a lighthearted and merry person. A Cardinal named Sforza had a fat little dog named Capricchio. Once the little dog met Filippo on the street. Animals tended to love and follow Filippo. Capricchio was no exception. Filippo used to pick up Capricchio and carry him around, as the little dog was too fat to walk very much. Then he made his disciples carry Capricchio. They didn't like that at all, as the dog was really funny looking, fat and losing his hair. The uglier Capricchio became, the more it amused Filippo to have his disciples carry him around. Cardinal Sforza was heard to complain, "He has taken my men away, and now he has even taken my dog!"

At a time when many people were filled with hate and narrowmindedness, Filippo Neri was full of love and goodwill toward all – Christians, Jews, and the other living creatures, great and small.

Juana and Saint Martin de Porres

How could he do it all, people wondered? The Dominican brother seemed to be in five places at once, caring for animals, nursing the sick, feeding the hungry, planting fruit trees along the roads for the needy, building shelters for orphans. He could not have done it without Juana.

Juana and Martin de Porres were the children of a Black woman, Ana Velasquez, who earned her living by washing clothes. Their father was a Spaniard. They were born in Lima, Peru. Martin was born in 1579, Juana a few years later.

Martin was apprenticed to a barber and learned barbering and surgery. Then he worked for a druggist and learned about herbs and medicines. At the age of 24, he went to a Dominican priory in Lima, swore his vows and received a brother's habit.

Martin was the infirmary supervisor who took care of the sick in the priory. He was a skillful and loving healer when a brother was sick. But he did more than care for the brothers of his own house. He went through the city of Lima, visiting the sick and injured and caring for them. If anyone needed extra care, he brought that person back to the priory and cared for them in his own cell. The sick began coming to the priory to seek his help, and soon it was full of sick people.

Some of the brothers objected to this. The superiors of the priory, too, were afraid contagious diseases would spread through the priory. They ordered Martin to send the sick people away, in spite of his pleas.

Martin's sister Juana was married now. Out of her great love for him, and her compassion for the sick, she opened her house to Martin's patients, and let them come and live in it. Martin

Martin brings another sick dog to Juana's house

came to her house and tended them, and saw that they had everything they needed.

Sick people kept on coming to the priory, seeking Martin's help. Martin continued to take them in, even though he was disobeying his superiors. When the Prior heard about it, he scolded Martin, and said he was breaking the rules. Martin answered, "But, Father, charity knows no rules!"

Martin's loving care included the animals also. He took in many strays: dogs, cats, an old mule that had been turned out to die. He set the broken wing of a vulture and healed it. He healed a wounded deer and set it free, and for years afterwards it kept coming down from the hills to be fed and petted by Martin.

Now the other brothers became unhappy because the priory was turning into a hospital for sick animals, and they told Martin to move them out. Again he appealed to Juana, and again she responded with love and generosity. She let him move his "animal hospital" into a room in her house. It was terrible! The animals ran all over her house. Many of them were not housebroken, and they made a terrible mess. When Juana told Martin about it, he spoke to the animals. "Brothers, you must not be troublesome! He told them to stay in their own room, and not to run all over Juana's house, and to go outside, like good, housebroken animals, when they needed to. Somehow the animals understood and cooperated.

Sometimes Martin allowed the mosquitoes to bite him. He wanted to feed them because, "They too are God's creatures."

Martin kept all the sheets and bandages for the infirmary in his cell. Once a colony of rats got into these linens. They were ruining them, nibbling holes and soiling them.

Still, Martin would not allow anyone to kill the rats. He caught one rat in a trap that didn't hurt it. He picked it up and talked to it, saying, "Run away now, brother rat, and tell your companions that they are doing a lot of harm." He told the rat that he was sorry for them, and would not let them be killed, but that they must not harm the linen. He ordered them to go out into the garden, and promised to bring food out to them every day.

Amazingly, the rats did as he asked. They came out of the linen closet, and every morning they were all out in the garden. Every day he took food out to them, and a great tribe of rats came out to meet him.

Juana and Martin loved each other all their lives. Each was ready to help if the other needed something. A generous, joyful love filled this brother and sister, who cared for so many creatures.

Chu-hung

A man who had a tremendous role in popularizing the ideas of not-killing (pu-sha) and releasing life (fang-sheng) in China was the Buddhist monk Chu-hung.

He was born in Hangchow in Chekiang Province in 1535. He studied the Confucian and Taoist classical books, and then, in his teens, he began to study Buddhism. In 1566 he became a Buddhist monk. He travelled around China, visiting famous teachers. In 1571, he returned to his birthplace and settled down in a hut on Mount Yun-ch'i in Hangchow. There was an old ruined monastery there.

The farmers around Mount Yun-ch'i were suffering from a lack of rain, and also from the ferocious tigers that infested the area and attacked people. Chu-hung responded to the people's needs. First he prayed for rain, and rain fell shortly afterwards.

Then Chu-hung carried out a prayer service to transform the tigers so that they would no longer attack people. The prayer service, he said, was not only to make the tigers peaceful, it was intended to help all sentient beings, and bring about the happiness of the whole world. Chu-hung said that it succeeded in changing the tigers, and that they no longer attacked people. Chu-hung settled down in the old monastery. The grateful people repaired it for him. Other monks joined him and he became the abbot.

In those days there were often bad feelings between the different Buddhist sects, "Ch'an" (zen) and "Pure Land" Buddhism. Chu-hung was a Pure Land Buddhist, but he taught that the two schools reached the same destination by different roads. He also showed courtesy and good will toward Taoists and Confucianists.

Chu-hung helped organize lay Buddhist societies, where Buddhist people who were not monks or nuns could learn how to practice Buddhism in everyday life. He persuaded many of his followers to give money to build ponds for releasing life. His followers met regularly to hear the scriptures and to give money for buying captive animals to release.

Chu-hung wrote two famous essays, "On non-killing" and "On Releasing Sentient Beings". Chu-hung taught that it is not enough merely to refrain from killing, one must also positively protect living things. He said that animals value their lives just as humans do, and that releasing life accords with the will of heaven and the teaching of Buddha.

In his essay, "On Non-Killing", Chu-hung argued that the practice of killing and eating animals is a custom, not a necessity, and that it must be stopped. He showed people how they could start by giving up meat on some days and hope to gradually grow in compassion. He and his monks were vegetarians. They did not wear silk, either, because silkworms are killed in the making of it. Chu-hung strongly condemned methods of cooking that cause animals great pain, such as cooking crabs while they are alive.

Chu-hung also wrote a famous morality book, similar to the Taoist Kan-ying p'ien, with detailed rules for leading a good life. It has many suggestions for good deeds that can be done for both people and animals, and also a practical list of faults to avoid. He died in 1615, after a life spent spreading ideas of humanity and compassion in China.

Richard Martin protects a horse - forcefully

Richard Martin

Many of the people who worked for animals' welfare have been gentle and meditative.

Richard Martin was different. He was fiery and combative, energetic and impulsive. His nickname was "Hairtrigger Dick".

He was an Irish landowner and magistrate at the end of the 18th century. He was a member of the British Parliament from County Galway.

He was skillful with both sword and gun, and took part in several duels, which left large scars on his body.

As magistrate (judge) on his huge estate in Ireland, he had the power to enforce the law by sentencing people to jail. He could not stand cruelty to animals. He used to sentence farmers to jail if they were cruel to their beasts.

He was also concerned about the suffering of human beings. At that time, many crimes were punishable by death - not only murder but even theft. People could be sentenced to death for stealing fairly small amounts of money. Martin tried to make the law more humane. He introduced a bill into Parliament which would have changed the law, so that forgery would no longer be punishable by death. He also tried to get a law passed to provide a free lawyer for poor people when they were tried for crimes that might get the death penalty.

Richard Martin was successful in introducing the first animal protection law ever passed by the British Parliament.

When he introduced his bill - "Martin's Act" - into Parliament in 1822, he was treated with ridicule and mockery. When he got up to speak about the bill, some members started barking and meowing. He turned toward the noise and said, "If the person who has just insulted me will retire to the committee room I will explain the bill to him!". No one, looking at the powerful, angry man, dared admit to making the noise.

After the law was passed, Martin did not just sit back and hope someone would enforce it. Whenever he saw an act of cruelty to an animal on the London streets, he stopped and personally brought the guilty person to justice. The public was often angry at him. Sometimes the judges treated him scornfully and dismissed the case against the cruel person. But he never despaired and continued to work courageously for humane treatment of animals.

For example, he once prosecuted two men who had been savagely beating helpless, tied-up horses. He also prosecuted people who conducted bull-baitings. These were ugly sports in which bulls were tied up to be attacked by dogs until they were killed.

His friend and colleague in the humane movement, John Lawrence, said that Martin actually produced a change in the character of the rough population of London.

Martin joined with a group of like-minded people, in 1822, to organize a society to carry on the work of protecting animals. The Reverend Arthur Broome was the head of the new society. Several of the founding members were also active in the British anti-slavery cause.

Richard Martin worked selflessly in the humane cause until he died at the age of 80. His friend, King George IV, gave him the nickname by which he is still known - he was no longer "Hairtrigger Dick", but "Humanity Martin".

Felix Berenguer Marquina

The sport of bullfighting was apparently introduced into Spain in the 11th Century, possibly from North Africa. It was highly controversial and many people opposed it. Ferdinand and Isabella tried to abolish it, but found that it was too popular. Several later Spanish rulers tried also. Some of the Popes excommunicated people who took part in bullfights. Pope Pius V declared,

We regard these exhibitions where bulls and wild beasts are baited ... as contrary to Christian duty and charity ... and prohibit and forbid exhibitions of this kind.

The Spaniards who conquered Mexico brought bullfighting with them and established it in the new world. It took a lot of courage to oppose a popular sport like bullfighting, but there were brave people who did so.

One of these was the Viceroy Felix Berenguer Marquina. He was born in Alicante, in Spain, in 1738. He joined the navy when he was 16, and soon became a captain. In 1800 he became Viceroy (Governor) of Mexico, which the Spaniards, at that time, called New Spain. From the very day of his reception in Mexico, he forbade bullfights.

The people were attached to bullfights, and his stand made him very unpopular. His advisory council said they had to have a bullfight to raise money. The Viceroy paid the money himself out of his own pocket, but he would not permit a bullfight.

Once when he was away on a trip, people took advantage of his absence and put on a bullfight. When he got back, and found out that there had been a bullfight, he was furious, and he immediately issued a decree declaring the bullfight null and void!

Marquina was a very humane man in a lot of ways. He defended the rights of women. Women had been excluded from many profitable industries by the all-male guilds. Marquina strongly enforced the law that women were free to work at any labor they chose that their strength was equal to.

He had been a prisoner of war, and had known the misery of captivity. As Viceroy, he released the English prisoners that the Spaniards were holding. The English Governor of Jamaica, in return, released the Spanish prisoners that the English were holding.

Marquina ran an honest administration and did his utmost to help the people when they suffered under floods and earthquakes. He warned the Spanish government that greedy landowners were concentrating too much land in a few people's hands. He tried to prevent unemployment among miners and working people.

Felix Marquina was one of many brave and compassionate Hispanic people who worked to put a stop to bullfights. There are humane societies in both Spain and Mexico today which are carrying on this work. They ask people who travel to their countries not to go to bullfights, because the money that tourists spend for tickets is a major factor in keeping bullfights going.

Preachers and Pastors

Arthur Broome was a young priest of the Church of England when he gave up everything he had for the cause of animals. He joined Richard Martin, Louis Gompertz, the Jewish vegetarian, and a few others, in setting up the first Society for the Prevention of Cruelty to Animals, in 1822.

Broome was one of the lucky ones - in a time of widespread poverty, he had a "living" - a safe, lifelong income as a parish priest. He gave it up to work full time, without pay, for the SPCA. The SPCA was very poor, and couldn't pay its debts. Arthur Broome, as the Secretary of the SPCA, was thrown into a horrible debtor's prison. He was locked up until Richard Martin and Louis Gompertz paid the SPCA's debts and got him out.   He endured mockery, poverty and jail to serve the cause of animals. He died in 1837.

Even before there was an organized animal rights movement, in the preceding two centuries, a lot of clergymen did good work for the animal cause.

Henry More (1614-1687) did important work, because he combatted Rene Descartes' ideas about animals. Descartes was a great mathematician, but he had no understanding of animals. He taught that they are only machines, without souls, reason or feeling. He said that they do not experience pain, and that the cry of a suffering dog is just a mechanical noise like the creak of a wheel. This idea became popular and did enormous harm. Science was developing fast in the 17th century. Descartes' idea gave anybody who wanted to do cruel experiments on animals a complete excuse. Terrible suffering resulted.

Henry More and Descartes wrote letters back and forth and argued. More objected to Descartes' views on animals. He said that no one can prove that animals don't have souls, and enjoy life after death. He thought it possible and in accordance with the goodness of God. He said that people deny that animals have souls out of "narrowness of spirit, out of overmuch self-love, and contempt of other creatures".

More said that the world was not made for man alone, but that God intended that the other living creatures should enjoy themselves also. He taught that God loves the animals and takes pleasure in their happiness. More believed that humans were supposed to rule over the animals, but in a kindly way. He quotes the Bible, "The good man is merciful to his beasts". He said,

> I think that he that slights the life or welfare of
> a brute Creature, is naturally so unjust, that if
> outward laws did not restrain him, he would be as
> cruel to Man.

It was fortunate that Henry More opposed Descartes' views. He was a distinguished philosopher and a beautiful writer. Descartes' views became widespread and did a lot of harm, but More was able to persuade many people to take a different view.

A century later a Church of England priest, Humphrey Primatt, wrote a book called A Dissertation on the Duty of Mercy and the Sin of Cruelty to Brute Animals - a whole book, all about kindness to animals! Primatt was a caring, sensitive man. He also opposed slavery and the slave trade. Primatt said,

> Pain is pain, whether it be inflicted on man or
> beast. ... a man can have no natural right to abuse
> and torment a beast.

John Wesley (1703-1791), the founder of the Methodist churches, was a strong spokesman for kindness to animals. He urged people to educate their children to be compassionate to animals. He wrote,

> I am persuaded you are not insensible of the pain
> given to every Christian, every humane heart, by
> those savage diversions, bull-baiting,
> cock-fighting, horse-racing, and hunting.

The Duke of Wellington

William Harris was a big boy, old enough to leave home and go
away to boarding school. He was crying, and for a good reason.
He was just about to leave for school, and he hadn't been able
to find anyone who would take care of his pet toad for him. He
was desperate. They would not allow him to bring the toad with
him to the school.

England's greatest general, the Duke of Wellington, happened
to come along.   He asked William what was wrong, and when he
heard, he agreed to take the toad until William got back home
for vacation. During the school term, he wrote five letters to
William, telling him that his toad was alive and well.

Wellington was a brilliant general and a powerful politician,
the conqueror of Napoleon, a man of force and determination, who
could be ruthless. But somewhere in his character he had an
element of goodness and gentleness that led him to do this kind
act for a boy and his toad.

Rabbi Israel Salanter

Many stories are told about Rabbi Israel Salanter, who lived
in Eastern Europe in the 19th century. He was noted for his
active compassion. Once, when he lived in Kovno, he found out
that the town poorhouse was appallingly bad. The poor people
who were forced to live there were sleeping on the ground in
filth. The Rabbi left the house of study, and went and lay down
on the ground among the poor. The supervisor of the poorhouse
was shocked to find him there. The townspeople begged him to
leave, but he refused to go until the place was repaired and
made fit for human beings.

Once, on the eve of Yom Kippur, the congregation waited and
waited, but Rabbi Salanter did not arrive at the customary time
to say the Kol Nidre prayer. They knew that he would not fail
to be present, on that solemn holy day, and they grew very
worried. A search party finally found the Rabbi. He had
rescued a lost calf, and was leading it home to its barn. To
Rabbi Salanter, the needs of the little animal came before even
the most sacred ceremonial observances of religion.

Many Jewish people, inspired by the humane teachings of
Judaism, have been active in the humane movement. Louis
Gompertz, one of the founders of the English SPCA, was one of
them.

Anna Sewell

A little Quaker girl, Anna Sewell, lived in a modest stucco
house in the London suburb, Hackney. The family had a small
income, lived and ate simply, and did their own washing.

One day a man was out shooting birds for fun.   He   shot   a
blackbird, which fell into the Sewell's front garden. He came
to get the bird. Nine year old Anna came to the door. He asked
for the bird, but left in a hurry when the quiet, polite Quaker
girl declared, "Thee cruel man, thee shan't have it at all!"

Anna and her brother Phillip grew up in the Quaker tradition
of simple living, honesty, and the duty to care for others.
Quakers worked vigorously to change society and provide for all
needy people.   They also taught "a tender consideration for the
creatures of God". Quakers would not hunt, or take part in any
"distressing of beasts for amusement". They were careful not to
overwork their animals, and to consider their feelings.

Anna Sewell writes "Black Beauty"

During the terrible potato famine in Ireland, Mary, Anna's mother, had been saving pennies for months for a trip to the seashore. When they heard of the starvation in Ireland, Mary told Anna and Phillip that she wanted to send money to help provide food, but the only money she had was the savings for the trip. The children instantly asked her to send it to Ireland.

Anna's family, the Sewells, were active in many humane causes. They fought the slave trade and the death penalty. They founded schools so that young ex-convicts could get education and jobs. They visited jails and slums. Anna's mother never had a trained cook. She always took an untrained poor woman or ex-convict, trained her to be a good cook, and got her a good job as a cook. Then she started all over with another untrained woman.

Anna Sewell grew up with the same active, caring attitude. When the family lived in a coal mining area of Gloucestershire, she started a Working Man's Institute where she taught night classes for miners and laborers - many of them could not read, and passionately wanted to learn.

All her life, she could not stand cruelty to an animal, and she interfered forcefully whenever she saw it.

She had a special love for horses. She rode and drove expertly. One of her friends told how gently she drove, never using the whip, and using the reins very lightly. Mostly, she talked to her horses and they responded to her voice. "Now thee must go a little faster - thee would be sorry for us to be late at the station", she said to one horse, who promptly speeded up.

Anna Sewell became an invalid in later years, and could not move around much, but near the end of her life, she did a great thing for horses.

She knew how to manage horses so that they enjoyed a happy life. She detested the mistreating of horses by overwork or beating. She hated the "check-rein" a rein that held the horse's head in an unnatural and painful position. People used them because they thought horses looked handsomer that way.

She wrote a book, "Black Beauty". It was published in 1877. It let readers experience what a horse feels in its life. It created great sympathy for horses. The book is one of the world's best sellers - around 30 million copies have been sold. "Black Beauty" changed people's ideas and led to the disuse of the check-rein. The quiet Quaker woman educated millions in "tender consideration for the creatures of God."

Black Beauty has continued popular and influential over the years. In an unusual court sentence, a Texas cowboy, in 1924 was convicted of cruelty to his pony. He was sentenced to a month in jail, and ordered to read "Black Beauty" at least three times.

Frances Cobbe

Rene Descartes spread his idea that animals are only machines in the 17th century. This attitude was widespread by the 19th century. One result was the practice of vivisection. Vivisection literally means cutting a living being, but it is used to mean using a living animal in any painful or harmful experiment. In the centuries after Descartes wrote, vivisection became widespread.

Many good people objected to this. The English writer, Samuel Johnson, denounced the "horrid operations" of vivisection. The great French writer, Victor Hugo, detested vivisection so much that he founded France's first anti-vivisection society and served as its president.

But the persons who did the most to make the European public aware of the vivisection problem were two Englishwomen, Frances Cobbe and Anna Kingsford.

Frances Cobbe was a very idealistic young woman. She worked hard in the slums of Bristol, in one of the "ragged schools" which gave poor children a chance for education. Then she injured her ankle, and went to Italy to recover.

That was where she first found out about vivisection. She was living in Florence, and she discovered that a scientist there, Professor Schiff, was treating his experimental animals with abominable cruelty. His Italian neighbors complained to the police, who did what they could. They put some tortured animals out of their misery. But there were really no laws against cruelty to animals at that time, so they could not do much.

Frances Cobbe wrote a protest, and 783 people signed it, both Italians and English residents of Florence. Schiff treated the protest with contempt. Then his neighbors sued him in court, claiming that the moans and cries of the animals in his lab were a nuisance to them. Schiff finally gave up and moved to Switzerland. He was afraid that he might suffer violence from his Italian neighbors, because they were so angry about his mistreatment of animals.

After this, Frances Cobbe returned to England and became a journalist. She found out that a lot of cruel experiments were being done in England. She tried to get the RSPCA to take action to stop it, but they could not agree on whether to act on animal experiments or not. So Frances Cobbe decided to take up the cause herself.

A doctor named George Hoggan had spent four months in Paris, as a student in the lab of Claude Bernard, the most infamous and pitiless of the experimenters on animals. Hoggan wrote letters to newspapers telling of the shocking things he had seen.

He and Frances Cobbe started a new organization to combat vivisection. They published a magazine, "The Zoophilist" (Greek for "The Animal Lover"). The society grew rapidly, and people of many different religions joined it. They tried to get Parliament to pass a bill to protect animals from suffering in scientific experiments, but they did not succeed. But they made the public aware of the issue, and were pioneers in the long fight to protect animals from cruelty in scientific experiments. This fight is still going on today, and dozens of animal rights organizations are carrying on Frances Cobbe's work.

Anna Kingsford is horrified at what she hears

Anna Kingsford

Anna Kingsford was born in 1846. She lived in the countryside in southern England, and loved riding and fox hunting. One day, riding home from a fox hunt, she had a vivid experience of the feelings of the terrified fox, almost as if she were the fox. Her attitude changed, and she quit fox hunting and became a vegetarian.

She married Algernon Kingsford when she was 21. She bought a newspaper, The Lady's Own Paper. As editor, she worked for the rights of women. Frances Cobbe wrote articles for the paper about women's rights. Anna Kingsford heard about the cruelties of vivisection from Frances Cobbe. The Lady's Own Paper began to publish articles about cruelty to animals also.

Anna Kingsford wanted to find out the truth about vivisection in medical research. She also wanted to learn medicine to investigate the healthfulness of a vegetarian diet. She decided to get medical training.

No English medical school accepted women at that time, so she went to France, where a woman could get a medical degree. She was one of the first Englishwomen to do so.

Many of the professors were hostile to her because she was a woman. A professor she called "G" refused to say her name when he called the role of the class, saying she was neither a man nor a woman. There was a 10 year old boy in one of the wards. He was deaf and unable to speak, but he knew sign language. He had an infected abcess on his shoulder, and he was unhappy of the bad smell of the abcess and of the evil smelling ointment they used on it. One day Anna Kingsford brought him a bunch of violets, so he would have a sweet fragrance to smell. When Professor "G" led his students through the hospital on his rounds, he saw the boy, sitting up smiling and holding the flowers. When he found out who had given the boy the violets, he changed his opinion of Anna Kingsford. "So!" he said, "she is a woman after all. Only a woman would have thought of bringing flowers to a sick child in the wards!"

In the medical school, the professors tried to pressure her to do painful experiments on animals, but she totally refused. Although she would not do them herself, she suffered great anguish over the cruelties she saw and heard. The worst researcher she knew of was Claude Bernard, who practiced every kind of needless cruelty, including slowly baking dogs to death while he watched.

When Anna Kingsford heard of this, she jumped up, in agony and rage, and prayed for the wrath of God on the man. She had one very wild and far-out idea. She believed that a person, if deeply moved, could launch his or her soul through space like a weapon, and destroy another person by sheer will power. In her horror at Bernard's cruelty, and her desire to stop it, she tried to do this. She tried to hurl her whole being through space to strike him, and then she fell back, exhausted. As it happened, Claude Bernard became sick and died shortly afterwards. That convinced her that the system worked.

After she completed her medical training, Anna Kingsford returned to .England, where she did an enormous amount of good work in educating the public about the realities of vivisection and the philosophy of kindness to all living things. She was for many years the president of the London branch of the Theosophical Society, and the Theosophical movement strongly supported and advocated her anti-vivisection views.

Although we do not believe that she really harmed the vivisectionist through will power, we can understand the feelings that made her depart from her normal humane and life-respecting principles in making the attempt. This dedicated, passionate woman did what she did, not because she wanted the vivisectionist to die, but because she felt that she must do something to protect helpless animals from treatment so cruel that she could not bear to hear of it.

Henry Bergh

Peasants in 19th century Russia lived a brutal life. They were poor, struggling hard for food and clothing, and they lived in fear under a tyrannical rule.

Like many people who are treated harshly themselves, they were often rough and cruel to their animals. If anyone tried to interfere with them, they would turn on him violently.

One man took the risk. He was a young American, Henry Bergh. He worked for the American legation in St. Petersburg, the Russian capital. When he saw horses mistreated in the streets, he rushed over and put a stop to it. He was able to overawe the rough peasants by his official-looking uniform and forceful manner.

When he left Russia, he travelled to England, and met people in the humane movement there. When he came back to the United States, right after the Civil War, he wanted to start a Society for the Prevention of Cruelty to Animals in America. It took a lot of work, but in 1866 the New York legislature passed a law incorporating the American Society for the Prevention of Cruelty to Animals. Henry Bergh was the President.

He was able to get a law passed against cruelty to animals in the state of New York.

There were no buses or cars in those days. Most people got around the city on big streetcars, which were pulled by horses. At rush hours, the streetcars were overloaded, often with far more people than the horses could possibly pull. The drivers would whip the horses and try to force them to pull the heavy cars. Henry Bergh took a very active part in fighting this evil. He frequently stood in the path of overloaded streetcars, to save the exhausted horses. Sometimes he was surrounded by crowds of angry people who cursed and threatened him, but he would not budge. He would not let the streetcar go until it was unloaded, and carried only the legal number of people, which the horses could pull.

Bergh also stopped carts and wagons that were overloaded. The men driving the wagons were furious at him. One waggoner attacked him and hit him with an iron bar.

Henry Bergh carries a child into court

The list of cruelties that Bergh fought is amazing. He opposed bullfighting, cockfighting, hunting, docking horse's and dog's tails, cruelty in slaughtering and in transporting animals, the use of the check-rein, pigeon shooting, "ratting" in which dogs were turned loose on captive rats, dogfighting, and vivisection.

He helped to get the United States Congress to pass a "Twenty-four hour law", which required anyone who transported animals by railroad to give them rest, food, and water once every twenty-four hours.

Up to this time, horses that fell down in the streets, injured or sick, were just left in the streets to die. Henry Bergh designed and built a special ambulance to carry them to a veterinary hospital for treatment. He also opened up his country property as a refuge for old horses.

There were no laws against cruelty to children at the time. People saw Henry Bergh's success in protecting animals from cruelty, and they began to appeal to him to help in cases of cruelty to children. In 1871 he intervened for the first time to protect a little girl who was being brutally beaten. The court found the woman who was beating the child guilty, and she was placed in her grandmother's care for safety.

In 1875 a church worker named Etta Wheeler tried to rescue a little girl who was being beaten by a stepmother. The door was slammed in her face, and the police would not act. She appealed to Henry Bergh. He sent two officers of the SPCA. They invaded the stepmother's home and picked up the little girl, Mary Ellen. She was covered with welts and wounds and badly starved. Henry Bergh carried the little girl into court and spoke for her. "The child is an animal", he said, and demanded that the little girl have at least the rights of an animal, and not be abused. He won the case, the child was taken away from the cruel family, and sent to a safe home. The woman who had beaten her was sentenced to a year in jail. Etta Wheeler afterwards adopted Mary Ellen.

This case opened people's eyes to the need for a society to protect children. The first Society for the Prevention of Cruelty to Children was founded in 1875, by Henry Bergh and two other men. Bergh served as its vice-president, and gave it office space in the SPCA building as long as it needed it.

Doctor Belisario Dominguez

The noblest of Mexico's opponents of bullfighting was Dr. Belisario Dominguez. He was born in Comitan de las Flores in the state of Chiapas in the south of Mexico in 1863. He studied medicine in Paris and became an outstanding doctor. He returned to his native town, where he was loved for his generosity in providing free medical care for the poor.

Dr. Dominguez was concerned with the backwardness and poverty of his native state, Chiapas. He had printed some flyers in which he boldly attacked the indifference and exploitiveness of the government. It took a very brave man to do this in Mexico in 1903, under the undemocratic government of Porfirio Diaz.

Dr. Dominguez soon decided that he needed a newspaper of his own if he was really going to reach people and change their thinking. So in 1904 he founded his own newspaper, which he called EL VATE, from an ancient Roman word meaning a poet or seer. He liked the word Vate because it was made of the first letters of the words valor (courage), alegria (joy), trabajo (work) and estoicismo (stoicism, endurance). These four things were the basis of his philosophy.

Belisario Dominguez had a vivid spiritual life and felt an identity with all living things. He looked with compassion on the defenceless animals. He used his newspaper to try to persuade his fellow citizens to abandon the needless cruelty of bullfighting. His descriptions of bullfighting are moving and terrible:

> The enthusiasm peaks; the bull bellows with pain and frenzy. The horse shakes in the convulsions of death. Music exalts the spirit, and the public, full of glee and satisfaction, applaud with frenzy, and demand with loud shouts "Another horse!" and then "Another!", "Another!" "Another!". They never tire of this. The bull has already killed several horses.

Dr. Dominguez said that horses and bulls are domestic animals, which serve man, and that man commits treason against them by having them killed in the bullfight. In one issue of El Vate he makes a moving appeal to people who go to bullfights:

> Mexicans! Spaniards! To you, to all the Spanish-American people who continue to enjoy the bullfight as a diversion, I appeal: reflect for one instant, and surely that instant of reflection will make sentiments of good will, generosity, and sweetness shine in you, such as are proper to your character, and then you will renounce these diversions.

Dr Belisario Dominguez gives out "El Vate" outside a bull ring

In another issue of El Vate, he expresses his compassion for the horses killed in bullfights, and writes an article as though the horse himself were talking to the people at the bullfight. The horse describes his long service to a human owner:

Young and vigorous, I was your faithful friend, your true servant, your inseparable companion. I helped you accumulate your fortune and shared your work with you, your weariness and your danger. Old, I was the delight of your children, I felt proud and happy to be able to carry them on my back. ... Now that I am wasted and decrepit, you think it right to amuse yourself and your children, seeing my tired and trembling body mangled. ... after you have amused yourself with my torture, recover your calm for a moment and think well about what you are doing.

In 1913, the elected government of Mexico was overthrown by the treacherous and murderous Victoriano Huerta. Huerta captured and murdered the humane and idealistic President, Francisco Madero, and Vice President Suarez. He began a reign of terror. Hundreds of innocent people were killed, including the Governor of Chihuahua, members of the Senate and Chamber of Deputies, and anyone who was suspected of opposing Huerta.

Dr. Dominguez did not want to be active in politics. It was not the field he wanted to work in. He had refused to be nominated for Senator. But in 1912 he accepted election as "Senador Suplente", a "substitute senator", which was supposed to be an honorary position, unless the acting Senator died or was unable to serve. In 1913, the acting Senator was killed in Huerta's bloodbath. Dr. Dominguez felt that it was his duty to serve. On September 23, 1913, he stood up in the Senate and, with incredible courage, tried to persuade his fellow senators to take action, and remove from office the murderer, Huerta, who had killed the lawful President. The Senators listened, terrified. Dr. Dominguez had his speech printed and distributed throughout the city, trying to rouse the citizens. He was arrested, and several days later his body was found.

The Congress was now roused to denounce Huerta for this murder and the disappearance of several others of their members. The country was aflame with anger. Huerta was overthrown and exiled by July of the next year.

Dr. Dominguez' memory is revered in Mexico. His native town, Comitan de las Flores is now Comitan de Dominguez. In 1953 the Mexican Senate established the Medal of Honor, Belisario Dominguez. It is a gold medal with a portrait of Dr. Dominguez. It is awarded annually to Mexican men or women who have distinguished themselves in the service of Mexico or of humanity. The year 1963, the hundredth anniversary of his birth, was declared the legislative year of Belisario Dominguez. In that year, also, his body was moved to Mexico's Rotunda de los Hombres Ilustres, the Rotunda of Illustrious Persons.

Anahareo

Anahareo was a young Iroquois woman of Canada, full of sensitivity to wild things. In 1925 she met a young Englishman who loved Indian ways, and had taken an Indian name, Grey Owl. She fell deeply in love with him and wanted to marry him.

But one thing caused her great anguish. Grey Owl was a professional trapper. He lived by setting out traps in the forest, travelling along his traplines to check his catch, and selling the fur from the trapped animals. Sometimes he found the fur animals dead, sometimes they were alive and starving. Often they had chewed off their own paws in their desperate desire to escape. Anahareo loved Grey Owl, but she begged and pressured him to stop inflicting torture and slow death on animals.

Grey Owl was a stubborn man. Anahareo knew that he would not change easily. For several years he seemed inflexible - but all the time his mind was changing, slowly and painfully.

For the first years of their life together, Anahareo, much as she hated it, helped Grey Owl with his trapping. It was their way of making a living. He noticed with wonder that the doomed trapped animals seemed to sense Anahareo's feeling for them. They looked toward her with appeal, and sometimes tried to crawl to her.

Then, in 1928, she set out a trap for a lynx. When she went back to check the trap, ten days later, she found a pitiful lynx in it. He had gnawed his trapped paw, trying to get free. He was starving, and had eaten all the bark off all the trees he could reach. When he saw Anahareo, he looked at her as if begging for help, as if he thought she had come to rescue him. Anahareo was horrified. She wanted to let him go, but she could see that he was dying. She had to kill him. On that day she made a decision. She never set another trap.

But she still could not persuade Grey Owl to stop trapping. But some of the things he saw in his work as a trapper made a deep impression on him. One was the time he came upon a mother beaver who was caught by one paw in a trap, moaning with pain, but holding one of her kittens in her other paw and nursing it. Grey Owl set her free. He came on animals caught in spring-pole traps, which he detested and would not use. These traps jerk the animal up in the air, where it hangs by one paw until it dies of hunger and thirst. Grey Owl was more and more troubled by the cruelty of trapping, but he repressed his thoughts, closed his mind, and went on trapping.

That winter the trapping was poor. Grey Owl had little fur to sell. He didn't make enough money to live on until the next winter.

Anahareo insists on saving the beaver kits

He decided to do some spring trapping, something he disapproved of and had never done before. Good trappers didn't trap in the spring when young beavers are born. He was uncomfortable, but he went ahead.

After he had set a trap for a mother beaver, he saw two tiny beaver kits swimming along. He raised his gun to shoot them. Anahareo cried, "Let us save them! It is up to us after what we have done!" Grey Owl agreed. They grabbed the tiny, half-pound creatures and put them in their boat.

The kittens were friendly and trusting. Anahareo and Grey Owl fed them canned milk. The beavers wanted to be picked up and petted a lot. They liked to sleep draped around the human's necks, inside their sleeves, or inside their shirt fronts.

Living with the beaver kittens completed the change in Grey Owl. He was already opposed to the wholesale trapping of beavers, because it was wiping the animals out. But this was different. He discovered that the beavers had feelings and could express them. They were affectionate, they experienced happiness and loneliness. "Why, they were little people!" he said, in one of his books. He was getting close to a decision to give up trapping beavers, although it was his main source of income. "To kill such creatures seemed monstrous" he said.

He told Anahareo, "I'm off the beaver hunt for good."

Instead, he wanted to set up a protected beaver colony and encourage them to multiply. He also wanted to work for legal protection for beavers so they could make a comeback. He still intended to hunt and trap other animals.

They built a cabin at Birch Lake in Ontario. They lived their with their two beavers, now grown to 15 pounds, who they had named McGinty and McGinnis. When Grey Owl built the cabin, it was winter and freezing cold. He brought in a pile of frozen moss and put it by the stove to thaw. He intended to use it to "chink" the logs of the cabin – that is, to fill the spaces between the logs to make the cabin warm.

When they woke up the next morning, they found that the beavers had taken the moss and done a pretty good job of chinking the spaces between the logs, as high as they could reach! Beavers are great builders, and are used to plugging up holes and cracks to keep their houses warm.

Grey Owl built a nice table for Anahareo and himself to eat on. The beavers were fascinated with the table top, which was out of their reach and seemed to have a lot of good smelling food on it. One night Anahareo and Grey Owl stayed away overnight. When they got home, the beavers had found a way to explore the unreachable table top. They had chewed the legs right off so it ended up on the floor!

Living with the intelligent, trusting beavers totally changed Grey Owl. He gave up all trapping, and became a government naturalist, a famous writer, lecturer and movie maker. He wrote of the wilderness and its beauty, and the need to protect it. He told of the life of the wilderness animals, their intelligence, affection and courage. He wrote of the cruelty of trapping and the vanishing of many kinds of animals. The professional trapper had become a voice for animals.

Anahareo and Grey Owl lived in the woods and tamed many other animals - muskrats, birds, squirrels and even a moose. And at the root of all the good work they did for animals was the loving, compassionate spirit of Anahareo - and the charm of two obstreperous beaver kittens.

Albert Schweitzer treats people and animals in his jungle
hospital

Albert Schweitzer

When Albert Schweitzer was an old man, in his jungle hospital in Africa, he told a story from his childhood.

He lived in the Alsacian countryside, in Germany, around 1900. When he was eight years old, he and his cousin Henry made slingshots which could shoot small stones.

One day Henry wanted Albert to go up the mountain with him to shoot birds. Albert hated the idea, but he didn't want to be laughed at, so he went.

They came to a bare tree, full of singing birds. Henry took aim and was about to shoot. The church bells rang just then, and the music of the bells mingled with the singing of the birds. Albert threw down his slingshot and scared the birds away. He later wrote that at that moment he heard, in his heart, the commandment, "Thou shalt not kill."

Albert grew up to become a gifted musician and a famous philosopher. In his twenties, he decided to become a doctor. He decided to leave his promising career in Europe, and to go start a hospital in the African jungle, to serve people who didn't have any medical care.

Albert Schweitzer developed the philosophy of reverence for life. He promoted it in his books, and lived it in the hospital at Lambarene.

The hospital was full of animals of all kinds. Everyone knew that Dr. Schweitzer would always take in any sick or hurt or orphaned animal. There were pelicans, owls, eagles, antelopes, chimpanzees and wild pigs.

Visitors who reached over to brush an ant off Dr. Schweitzer were stopped with "No, no, that's my ant!"

Sometimes he was seen sitting, writing prescriptions with one hand, unable to use the other hand because his kitten had gone to sleep with its head on his hand, and he would not disturb it.

Albert Schweitzer gave himself to serve. He served human beings in his hospital, repaired injuries, cured diseases, and cared for incurably sick people, including many lepers. He loved and cared for many animals. And through his books and his teaching, he spread the idea of reverence for life all over the world.

Mahatma Gandhi

He may be the greatest human being of the 20th century. He was certainly the greatest teacher of ahimsa. He put ahimsa into practice to make huge changes in the world, as no other person in our century has done.

Two things were outstanding in Gandhi's practice of ahimsa. First, he could resolve bitter and violent conflicts, that looked impossible to cure. He invented a way of making ahimsa very powerful and very practical. He called it satyagraha (literally truth-force). Using satyagraha, people stand up strongly for their rights and refuse to yield to injustice. They do this without violence. They regard the oppressor with love, and appeal to his or her conscience. If jailed, injured, or even killed, the satyagrahi (person who does satyagraha) suffers without hatred.

Gandhi used satyagraha to combat injustice many times. He did it as a young Hindu lawyer in South Africa, resisting unjust racial laws. His great satyagraha campaigns for Indian self rule finally persuaded the British to abandon their undemocratic rule over India.

Gandhi also used a form of non-violent persuasion when he fasted. When the city of Calcutta was torn by violent riots and killings in 1947, Gandhi went there. He announced that he would fast unto death unless Calcutta became peaceful. His fast drew people of all groups together, and in two days the city was peaceful. It continued to be so, even in next few years when the rest of India was filled with riots and killings.

In 1932, when Gandhi was in jail for his activities in favor of self-rule for India, he decided to fast against the untouchable system. Untouchables were a very poor group of outcasts in India. They were barred from good jobs, from using wells, temples, and many roads and streets. When Gandhi started his fast, thousands of temples all over India changed their policies, and began to welcome untouchables. Villages opened their wells, roads and streets to untouchables and passed "anti-untouchability resolutions". Gandhi ended his fast after 13 days. He had revolutionized Indian attitudes toward untouchables.

The second outstanding thing about Gandhi's practice of ahimsa is that he interpreted it to mean positive love and deep fellow feeling for all creatures.

Gandhi opposed the animal sacrifices which were made in some Hindu temples. He said that the life of a lamb is as precious as the life of a human being, and that the more helpless a creature is, the more it is entitled to protection.

A sick calf troubles Gandhi and Kasturbai

Like other Hindus, he believed in protecting cows.   But he disagreed with those fanatical Hindus who used the cow issue to stir up hatred for the Moslems, who ate beef.   Gandhi said that Hindus should improve their own treatment of cows.   He said that although Hindus would not kill cows, they often neglected and underfed them.   He said that Hindus should set a better example, and trust the Moslems to become more sensitive and considerate.

Gandhi and his family were vegetarians, and would not eat meat even when they were sick and their doctors said their lives depended on it.

Gandhi built an ashram, a place where he and his family and followers   could   live   together and practice self-sacrifice and service.   The land where they built was wild and rough and full of poisonous snakes.   Gandhi and his friends decided not to kill the snakes.   He felt this act of faith was justified, for in all the years they lived there, no one was ever hurt by a snake.

Gandhi acted on deep love, not the letter of the rules.   Once a calf in the ashram was very sick.   It had rabies and was suffering terribly.   Gandhi decided that, since they could not stop its pain, it should be mercifully put to death.   Gandhi's wife, Kasturbai, objected.   She objected to all killing, and killing a cow or calf was a serious sin to an orthodox Hindu like her.   Then, said Gandhi, she should go and care for the calf herself.   She went to do so.   She saw its agony, and understood Gandhi's compassion.   She agreed that he was right. A doctor ended its suffering with an injection.

Gandhi's life was spent in trying to build a just and peaceful society.   He did so much that it is impossible to tell it all.   In 1948 he was killed by a fanatical Hindu who objected
to Gandhi's work for peace with the Moslems of India.
His teachings live on. They have inspired
millions all over the world. His ideas
were adopted by Dr. Martin Luther
King. King, like Gandhi, led
a far reaching revolution,
non-violently and
with
love.

Audrey

The baby monkeys had been taken from their mother at birth.
Then they were put in solitary confinement in isolation cages.
They were totally deprived of mother love and care. They were
not allowed to touch or interract with any living thing.

This kind of experiment has been done many times. The effect on the monkey is very terrible. Monkeys are intelligent animals. They are very social animals. If they are isolated they become very unhappy. They sit and rock endlessly. Some scream constantly. They are damaged for life. They behave like insane people. They never learn to play with other monkeys. They never mate or raise babies. Some of them die from the stress and loneliness.

Audrey was an education student in a university. She had a job in the research lab where the baby monkeys were kept. The researcher planned to keep them in isolation for two years. Audrey could not stand it. She knew that baby animals need mothering and social life. So every night, when she went in to do her caretaking work in the lab, she got the six little monkeys out of their isolation cages. She sat on the floor and played with them.

One night the head experimenter walked in. He saw Audrey sitting among the monkeys. They were having a wonderful time, playing with her and with each other. The researcher was very angry.

Audrey stood up, also angry, and told him that it was improper and immoral to blight the development of young animals that way. The researcher said that he felt some respect for her, although she had spoiled his experiment. She was never allowed to play with the baby monkeys again.

The story of experiments on animals today is a very sad one. Many experimenters do experiments like the one Audrey spoiled, depriving animals of all the things that give them happiness. Many experiments inflict great pain and harm on animals. Hundreds of thousands of animals are used in experiments every year. There is no adequate system of control to make sure that animals do not suffer unnecessary pain, that their living conditions are humane, or that the experiment is really useful. (Many of the worst experiments are pointless, or are repetitions of experiments that have often been done before.)

Many good animal rights organizations are trying to improve this terrible situation. You will see the names of some of them in the appendix to this book.

One bright spot in this story is Audrey, a brave, warm-hearted teacher in training. She responded to six baby monkeys as living fellow creatures, not as things to use unfeelingly in a lab. She was ready to risk losing her job and her income to give them a little play and affection.

Velma Johnston watches over the wild horses

Velma Johnston

Horses originally evolved in North America, but the horse was extinct in America when Columbus arrived. America's wild horses are descended from the horses the Spaniards brought from Europe, with additions from horses that have excaped from other farmers, settlers and explorers. By 1850 there were at least 2 million wild horses roaming the western United States.

At the end of the 19th century, "Cattle Barons" began to pasture huge herds of cattle on the western plains. They killed off all the wild horses they could find, to make more room for their cattle. (They did the same to the buffalo).

In 1934, Congress set up the Bureau of Land Management. Unfortunately, the Bureau had a strong bias against wild horses, and had a policy of killing and removing wild horses from federal lands in the west. They allowed dog food canners to round up and slaughter huge numbers of wild horses.

In 1950, a Nevada ranch owner, Velma Johnston, was driving along highway 395 on her way to Reno. She saw a truck carrying live animals, with blood leaking out of it. She followed it, and when it stopped, she saw that it was full of captured wild horses, terribly injured and wounded. She asked the driver what had happened, and he told her that the horses had been "run in" by plane. (Many wild horse hunters chase the horse herds in airplanes, flying low and shooting the horses to drive them toward the waiting trucks.)

Mrs. Johnston said, "I knew I couldn't live with myself unless I did something about it." She set to work to protect wild horses from cruelty and extermination.

Velma Johnston is responsible for getting a wild horse protection law passed in Nevada. She was also the driving force behind the federal "Wild Horse Annie bill" (1959) which prohibits running down wild horses by airplane on federal lands.

She also founded the Wild Horse Organized Assistance, Inc. (WHOA!) of Reno, Nevada, which works for the protection and humane treatment of both wild horses and wild burros, and has done a lot of good work.

The nickname "Wild Horse Annie" was given to Velma Johnston, in mockery, by her opponents, but she accepted it as a badge of honor. Mrs. Johnston has done a great job of organizing support for horses and burros, and informing the public about what was happening to them.

Author Marguerite Henry wrote a moving children's book, "Mustang: Wild Spirit of the West", which tells about Velma Johnston's campaign.

Jane Goodall

An English schoolgirl in Bournemouth started her own "Natural History Museum, Open to the Public, All Contributions for Old Horses".

And there you can see both sides of Jane Goodall's passionate attachment to animals.

In her childhood, she loved animals, and had an intense desire to learn about them. She walked the cliffs, and watched mammals, birds, and insects, and wrote down what they did. She often said that when she grew up she was going to Africa to study animals.

When she was nine, her mother took her to a lecture by a man who had a golden eagle. When he asked if anyone wanted to handle it, Jane was out in front at once.

She wrote a magazine for children, called "The Alligator", full of information about animals.

The other side of her passion for animals shows in "All Contributions for Old Horses". It was very typical that she sent the money she received from the museum to a fund for old horses. She has deep sympathy for animals, and has often gone to great lengths to help an animal in trouble.

Jane Goodall is famous for her discoveries about chimpanzees. In 1960 she went into the forest at Gombe in Tanganyika in east Africa. She lived there for several years. Her mother was with her part of the time, but for a long time she was entirely alone in the forest.

The wild chimps avoided humans, but Jane Goodall, with her patient and sensitive ways, slowly won their trust and got close to them.

She was able to move among them and observe many things never seen by human beings before. She discovered the fact that chimpanzees make and use tools. She saw them chew up leaves to make sponges to sop up water that was out of reach of their mouths, down in hollow logs. She saw them strip the leaves off small stems to make tools to catch termites out of termite nests. She was the first person to observe chimpanzees forming hunting parties and hunting other mammals.

The chimps became more and more trusting and friendly. They let her touch them and even play with their babies.

Hugo van Lawick, an animal photographer, came to Gombe to photograph the chimps. He and Jane Goodall were married.

The saddest thing
that happened during
their years at Gombe was a
polio epidemic among the chimps.
Six chimps died and nine were crippled.
Then Jane and Hugo van Lawick were able to
get polio vaccine. They fed it to the chimps.
Most of the chimps ate the vaccine-filled bananas
happily, but a few noticed the taste and spat out banana
and vaccine together. For these fussy eaters they fixed special
bananas with only one drop of vaccine on each one. And so they
got the whole troop vaccinated against polio.

109

The two humans cared for one old male chimpanzee, "Mr. McGregor", who was badly crippled by polio. At first he was afraid of them, but soon he sensed that they wanted to help, and he even let Jane Goodall pour water in his mouth when he was thirsty. They fed him and kept him clean. Once a group of big male chimps, upset and frightened by Mr. McGregor's illness, advanced to attack him. The van Lawicks stepped in front of him and faced the dangerous animals. Luckily, the charging chimps turned aside and left.

Finally, the sick chimp got worse, and the two humans had to face the fact that there was no hope, and that he was more and more miserable. Sadly, they fed him his favorite breakfast, then quickly and painlessly ended his life.

Another chimp, a female they called Gilka, developed a swelling on her nose. It grew until she could hardly breathe. They were able to shoot tranquilizer into Gilka and find out what was wrong. With the help of friendly veterinarians they got the right medicine and treated her.

Even after all the things they did to her to treat her disease, Gilka continued to trust the two humans.

Jane Goodall van Lawick has showed us that love and sympathy for animals can help the serious scientific investigator of animals. Many people studying primates today are indifferent to their feelings. They imprison them in small, boring concrete and steel cages, they deprive them of normal social life, and put them through painful experiments. But the woman who achieved the greatest breakthroughs in primate studies in this century worked with empathy and kindness.

Greenpeace

A Russian whaling ship was hunting, 60 miles off the coast of the United States, near the state of Washington. The year was 1975.

The hunt was interrupted when a little group of people in small, inflatable "Zodiac" boats got between the whales and the hunters. The whalers went ahead and fired their explosive harpoons' at the whales. The Greenpeace people in their fragile little boats ducked as the heavy explosive harpoons flew over them.

Greenpeace members have done this many times. Placing their boats, and their bodies, between the whaling ships and the whales has saved fin whales in Icelandic waters and off the coast of Spain (the Greenpeace ship was arrested and hauled into port both times). In 1982 six Greenpeace members chained themselves to a Peruvian whaling ship. They were arrested and charged with piracy. Greenpeace has not only done all these non-violent direct actions for whales, it has also informed and educated people about whales and whaling.

Greenpeace didn't start as an anti-whaling organization. It was started in 1970, in Vancouver, Canada. Its members were concerned over American nuclear testing in Alaska. Many citizens, both American and Canadian, joined the protest, and the tests were stopped in the following year.

Then in 1972, the ship Greenpeace III sailed to Mururoa Atoll in the South Pacific. The French government was testing nuclear weapons there, and Greenpeace went to protest. French troops attacked the Greenpeace III and beat the crew members. One young man was partially blinded by the attack.

The fragile rubber boat gets between the whales and the hunters

Many friends of animals detest the annual hunts of "whitecoat" (very young) baby seals. The hunt is particularly cruel because the babies are often killed in front of their mothers, who are unable to protect them from being clubbed to death and skinned. Greenpeace has been active in opposing the baby seal hunt. Greenpeace members in 1976 stood in front of baby seals and used their own bodies to protect them from hunter's clubs. In 1979, some Greenpeace volunteers chained themselves to sealing ships to stop the hunt. Greenpeace women volunteers have sometimes splashed green dye on the white coats of baby seals. This make their fur useless to the fur hunters, and so saves them from being killed. In 1982, after many protests from Greenpeace and other animal rights groups, the European Common Market banned the import of products made from the fur or skin of seal pups. This cut the demand for seal skins, so in 1983, only 35,000 baby seals were killed, instead of the quota of over 300,000. Greenpeace will continue to work on the seal hunt until the clubbing of baby seals is entirely stopped.

Greenpeace is still concerned about nuclear testing. The members want to protect the earth from nuclear pollution, and humankind from the danger of nuclear war. Greenpeace advocates the Comprehensive Nuclear test ban treaty as a step to control the arms race. Greenpeace is very active in fighting the dumping of both radioactive and toxic chemical wastes in the rivers, oceans and bays. They have exposed the dumping of dangerous radioactive wastes in Cumbria in northern England, and dangerous chemical wastes in Maryland, New Jersey and several other American states. Greenpeace members have placed themselves beside British navy ships which were trying to dump nuclear waste in the ocean in order to stop them.

Greenpeace is concerned with the whole earth. But the welfare of animals is a major part of their task. They have worked on the protection of dolphins, which are killed in large numbers by tuna fishermen, They work to protect many kinds of seals, not just the baby harp seals. They work to prevent wild orcas ("killer whales") from being captured for exhibition in shows. They have joined with concerned Alaskan citizens to protest the hunting of Alaskan wolves from airplanes and helicopters.

Greenpeace advocates saving lives by non-violent confrontations. In defending whales and seals, they take a risk themselves, but they do not hurt anyone. They also inform citizens and politicians of what is happening and try to work through the lawmaking and political process.

A Model SPCA

Most of this book is about people doing things for animals. But animals do things for people too.

The Society for the Prevention of Cruelty to Animals in San Francisco, California, has a "Hearing Dog" program. Abandoned dogs at their animal shelters are trained to work for deaf people, just as "Seeing Eye Dogs" work for blind people.

A deaf person can't hear people knocking on the door or ringing the doorbell. But if the person has a hearing dog, the dog tells the owner that there is someone at the door by running back and forth between the door and the person. If the telephone or smoke alarm bell rings, the dog runs between the person and the phone or smoke alarm. (Deaf people use special telephones called TTYs. They type their messages, and read the answer from a screen or paper tape.) A hearing dog alerted his owner to a burglary by running to the place where the burglar was breaking in. An unusually intelligent hearing dog has been trained to ride with its person in a car, and alert him if a siren sounds, from an ambulance or fire truck.

When the deaf person's alarm clock goes off in the morning, the hearing dogs jump on their persons' chests and lick their faces until they get up. (They usually get up quickly.)

Hearing dogs help deaf parents, by telling them when their baby is crying. The dog runs back and forth between the baby and the parents.

Hearing dogs are given, free, to people all over the state. The hearing dog program is a great thing. It helps deaf people to live independently, and it provides homes for abandoned dogs.

There are SPCA's in most cities all over the country. The San Francisco SPCA is an excellent one. It was founded in 1868, right after Henry Bergh founded the first American SPCA.

It has done an immense amount of work for animals over the years. It saved the city's police horses from being slaughtered when they got old. It provides a home for such old, retired horses at its Animal Home Farm.

It rescues and treats injured animals, wild or tame. If they are wild, it releases them again in a suitable place. It has rescued birds, seals, cats, dogs, rats, raccoons, and many other animals.

It was able to have the steel trap banned in San Francisco.

It takes reports of cruelty to animals, and, when necessary, rescues the animal and prosecutes the person who has committed the cruelty.

It takes in stray and unwanted animals and tries to find homes for them. It is able to find homes for 84% of its healthy animals - an outstanding success rate.

It educates people about the right treatment of animals, by radio and programs in schools. SPCA volunteers go into schools with educational materials and live animals, and teach children to have fellow-feelings for living things.

Most communities have a Society for the Prevention of Cruelty to Animals. An SPCA can be a good place to adopt a pet, to get help if an animal is abused or needs help, or to volunteer some time.

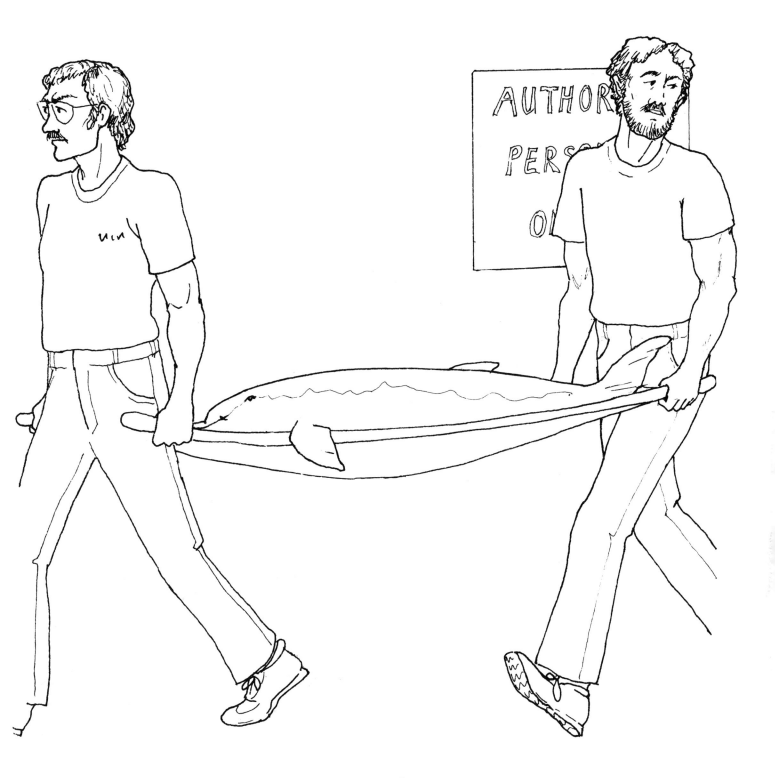

The Dolphin Rescuers

What could make two honest, intelligent, law abiding young men organize a break-in into a marine biology lab in the middle of the night? In that raid, on May 30, 1977, two female bottlenose dolphins, Puka and Kea, were taken out of their concrete isolation tanks, driven carefully in a padded van to the beach, and released in the Pacific.

The two men, Steven Sipman and Kenneth Le Vasseur, were serious, responsible persons who had been students in animal psychology. They knew a lot about dolphins. They knew that dolphins are very intelligent, affectionate, and social. They knew about the positive feelings that dolphins have for human beings. Dolphins have frequently rescued people who were in danger of drowning. Dolphins have visited beaches to play with humans, especially children. A dolphin will not hurt a human being. Some experimenters have deliberately hurt dolphins to provoke them to attack, but it is almost impossible to get a dolphin to attack a human.

Dolphins swim fast and far. They are unhappy in captivity, and often just give up and die, or beat their heads on the sides of their tanks until they die of the damage.

Steven and Kenneth were concerned about Puka and Kea. The dolphins were at the institute of Marine Biology of the University of Hawaii in Honolulu. They were kept in two separate isolation tanks, without any society. They weren't allowed the companionship of people or other dolphins. They were being used in behavioral experiments. They were overworked and their food rations had been reduced. Even their toys had been taken away. Puka was beating her head on hard objects in her tank until it was bloody, like those dolphins who are so unhappy that they kill themselves.

After the dolphins had been released, Steven Sipman and Kenneth Le Vasseur called a press conference, to announce that they had organized the rescue, and to make a plea for the right of dolphins to be free. They said that the only crime was keeping intelligent, social dolphins in solitary confinement for life.

The legal authorities cracked down hard on them. They were accused of committing a felony. The judge excluded much of the testimony about conditions in the lab, and about the intelligence and personalities of dolphins. Both men were convicted. One was sentenced to six months in jail, but on appeal this was reduced to four hundred hours of community service. Both men took an tremendous risk to save the dolphins. Their lives were seriously disrupted for several years, with the trials, appeals and costs. Thanks to their courage and compassion, Puka and Kea were released from miserable solitary confinement, and returned to freedom in the ocean.

There are many other dolphins that have been captured and are being held in conditions that frustrate all their instincts. Some are subjected to painful experiments. Many animal rights groups are trying to do something about this problem. It is very wrong for people to behave cruelly to dolphins, who never do anything but good to human beings.

Appendix: Some Organizations That Work For Animals

There are many fine organizations working for the welfare of animals. The following pages list some of them. There are many more good groups that we did not have space to list.

The reader may want to find out more about them, and then begin to support some of them by volunteering time or donating money. It is a good idea to subscribe to a good animal rights newsletter, so that you are informed about what is happening, and can do what is needed to help the cause. You might, for example, want to write to your legislators about laws to protect animals.

Agenda
P.O.Box 5234
Westport, CT 06881
    Agenda is an excellent newsmagazine. It covers the activities of many animal rights organizations and a wide range of issues. It is fair, well researched and really valuable for anyone who wants to be well informed on animal issues. It is published every other month. To subscribe, send a $15 check made out to Animal Rights Network, Inc. to the above address.

American Fund for Alternatives to Animal Research
175 West 12th Street, 16-G
New York, NY 10011
    AFAAR. is modelled on Britain's Air Marshall Lord Dowding Fund for Humane Research, which has been promoting non-animal research since 1973. AFAAR provides grants for non-animal research. AFAAR recently joined Beauty Without Cruelty in raising $200,000 to find a non-animal alternative to the cruel Draize rabbit eye test.

Animal Aid
111 High Street
Tunbridge, Kent TN9 1DL
    Animal Aid does educational, legislative and public information work.

Animal Protection Institute
P.O.Box 22505
Sacramento, CA 95822
    The A.P.I. works to end cruelty to pets, livestock and wildlife. It monitors ads for cruel products and informs the retail outlet or the magazine in which an ad for a cruel product appears. It has succeeded in getting chain stores to stop selling leghold traps and exotic pets. It does a fine job of reaching the general public through newspaper, radio and TV announcements. It conducts humane education and publishes a quarterly magazine, Mainstream.

Animal Welfare Institute
P.O.Box 3650
Washington, D.C. 20007
     The Animal Welfare Institute works for farm and lab animals,
wildlife and marine mammals.   It publishes an excellent
quarterly report.

Beauty Without Cruelty (U.S.A.)
175 West 12th Street
New York, NY 10011
     Beauty Without Cruelty keeps the public informed about the
suffering of animals in the fashion and cosmetic industries.
They suggest alternatives to fashion items involving cruelty.
They encourage makers of cosmetics and household products to
make their products without cruelty to any animal. They publish
a useful newsletter, The Compassionate Shopper, to enable the
consumer to find cruelty-free products.   Membership is $10,
members receive 3 copies a year of the newsletter.

Beauty Without Cruelty (United Kingdom)
11 Lime Hill Road
Tunbridge Wells, Kent, TN1 1LJ
     The British organization was the first in this field, and the
model for the American and other daughter societies.

British Union for the Abolition of Vivisection
143 Charing Cross Road
London WC2 HOEE

Canadian Federation of Humane Societies
101 Champagne Avenue
Ottawa K1S 4P3 Ontario

The Fund for Animals
140 West 57th Street
New York, NY 10019
     The Fund for Animals was founded in 1967 by Cleveland Amory.
Since that time, this fast-growing organization has acquired
200,000 members. It is active on the whole range of animal
issues.   Fund for Animals members were pioneers in the act of
painting baby seals with harmless dye, to make their fur useless
to hunters.   They have been active in wildlife defence,
opposition to bullfighting and rodeos, hunting and whaling. FFA
has filed lawsuits to defend animals, has rescued large herds of
animals which were faced with slaugher by the U.S. government,
and has led opposition to cruel research on animals. The fund
does a lot of educational work too. Student membership is $7,
adult $15. They have an excellent newsletter and also sell books
and other things.

120

Fund for the Replacement of Animals in Medical Experiments
312 Worpole Road
London SW20 8QU
   FRAME has been a pioneer in finding alternatives to the use of animals in scientific experiments.

Greenpeace USA
1700 Connecticut Ave, NW
Washington, DC 20070
   The activities of Greenpeace were described on pages 111-114.

Greenpeace (United Kingdom)
36 Graham Street
London N18 LL

The Humane Society of the United States
2100 L Street NW
Washington, DC 20037
   This large, energetic organization is active on a variety of fronts - state and federal legislation, vivisection, humane farming and slaughter. They are very active in the field of humane education. They publish a quarterly, Humane Society News, a young children's magazine, Kind, and many other publications. Membership is $10.

International Primate Protection League
P.O.Box 9086
Berkeley, CA 94709
   This league has done great work for primates, including opposing illegal and cruel capture and import practices and laboratory abuses.

Mobilization for Animals
P.O.Box 337
Jonesboro, TN 37659
   This is an activist organization which conducts demonstrations and direct action against cruelty to animals.

The National Anti-Vivisection Society
100 East Ohio Street
Chicago, IL 60611
   The NAVS works for the protection of animals used in experiments and testing. It is active in monitoring and promoting legislation as well as education and public information. NAVS publishes an excellent quarterly newsletter, the National Anti-Vivisection Society Bulletin. They offer for sale many books in the animal rights field. Membership is $10.

Royal Society for the Prevention of Cruelty to Animals
The Causeway,
Horsham, Sussex RH12 1HG

Society for Animal Rights
421 South State Street
Clarks Summit, PA 18411

Society for Animal Protective Legislation
P.O.Box 3719
Georgetown Station
Washington, DC 20007
   This group works on legislation for animals, as does the
following:

United Action for Animals
205 East 42nd Street
New York, NY 10017

Vegetarian Information Service
Box 5888
Washington, DC 20014
   This service promotes and informs about vegetarianism.

Vegetarian Society of the United Kingdom
Parkdale, Dunham Road
Altrincham, Cheshire WA14 4QG

To buy more copies of

FRIENDS OF ALL CREATURES

ask your bookstore ... or, order directly from

Sea Fog Press, Inc.
P.O.Box 210056
San Francisco, CA 94121-0056

enclose check or money order for $7.95 for each paperback
                              $12.95 for each hardcover
we pay postage
Californians add appropriate tax